IT'S WORTH A LIFE
Hearing and Responding to God's Call

Michael G. Cogdill

© 2017

Published in the United States by Nurturing Faith Inc., Macon GA,

www.nurturingfaith.net.

Library of Congress Cataloging-in-Publication Data is available.

ISBN 978-1-63528-012-8

Dedications

Dedicated to my family, especially to my grandchildren,
who I hope will always keep their hearts open to God's call,
and to all my students, past and present,
who have shared their call stories and journeys with me.
Thank you.

Contents

Foreword

The topic of God's call is a powerful and timeless one. I am proud that my father is writing about this important subject, because he is up to the task. I write not to extol my father's virtues but to add words of affirmation about his knowledge, passion, and dedication to this subject.

In this book, you will read about the dimensions of God's call, including lessons and insights about what we know regarding how and when God calls. You will notice similarities to your own experience. You will likely discover differences in how God has called you relative to others, since God's call is personal to our individual lives. You will be challenged to consider that God's specific call for each of us, and our response to that call, affects not only individuals, but families and generations.

I can testify to the generational impact of calling, because God's call to my parents has had a substantial influence on my career, ministry, and family. It is no accident that the calling and passion of my father's vocational life became the teaching and encouraging of young ministers. It is my belief that God ordained that calling before my father was born. Not always do we, God's children, get our calling right, but I believe that my father has.

You will read in my father's words an account of his personal calling. He will share the story of how that call was revealed to him and what happened in response. What he did not know at the time, and what is clear only in retrospect, is that God's call for his life would include being a preacher, professor, and encourager for young men and women for decades to come. This book contains not only his story but old and new examples of God's calling, all of which are a reminder of how great our God is.

As a brief word of testimony, I have experienced the highs and lows of the struggle to find and follow God's call. My first struggle with call came as a 22-year-old first-year law student. After a time of internal conflict, I turned to Dad for help. He did not rebuke me, lecture me, or command me. Instead he listened, encouraged, and loved me. That experience and process have led to nearly two decades of discussion between us about calling. Dad never pushed me to be a vocational minister. He never placed his own agenda or will on my life. Instead, God has used him as a constant source of support and affirmation, patiently observing as I have followed my own calling in law, ministry, and other areas. Today my call journey continues, and Dad continues to cheer for me and strengthen me, much like key people in your life and in the examples you will read in the pages ahead.

Thank you for reading this book. I hope that it will aid and inspire your own call journey as well as your role in assisting others. Above all, I pray that we all recommit to finding God's will in our lives and fulfilling the high calling of ministry in whatever form God intends for each of us.

Jason M. Cogdill
Winston-Salem, NC

Acknowledgments

I wish to thank several persons to whom I owe a debt of gratitude for their contributions to the publication of this book. First, I wish to thank Mr. Johnny Pierce and Dr. Tony Cartledge of Nurturing Faith Publishing, Inc., for their encouragement. Dr. Cartledge, my colleague at Campbell University Divinity School, provided valuable counsel and editing during the writing process. Special thanks are also extended to two other of my colleagues, Dr. Glenn Jonas and Dr. Barry Jones, for their encouragement to apply for a sabbatical leave, and to Dr. Jones for teaching two of my courses while I was away.

I am grateful to Campbell University for granting me a sabbatical leave during the fall semester of 2016. The writing of this book was my sabbatical project.

I am grateful to Louise Taylor, professor emeritus of English of Meredith College, for her valuable work in the editing of this manuscript. Her editing skills contributed significantly to the presentation of this book. Special thanks are also extended to Muriel Lasater, my excellent graduate assistant, for typing the manuscript.

Finally, I wish to thank my family for their interest, encouragement, and support of this project. I am proud to share the dedication of this book with them.

Introduction

For more than three decades, I have taught courses in undergraduate and graduate theological education in a church-related university. Included in these years has been an active ministry of interim pastorates, preaching, and service to local churches. At numerous times, students and laypersons of all ages and backgrounds have brought to me questions about and thoughts related to God's call.

Frequently, the concerns were expressed in this manner: "I want to do God's will for my life. I think I am feeling a call from God to enter vocational ministry. But how can I be sure?" At other times, the questions were posed this way: "If you are feeling a call from God, where do you begin? Do you tell your pastor or change your major to religion?" And occasionally, I have heard this concern: "I know for sure that God called me to the work of missions when I was younger. I did not act on the call then, but the conviction of God's call has never left me. Do you think it is too late to answer this call now?"

Questions such as these have motivated me to write this book. It seeks to provide a lighted path for those wanting to understand the various features of God's call.

This book is designed to reach multiple audiences. First, I hope it will be a resource for beginning classes in formal theological education. For students interested in church ministry, I believe an appropriate starting point for theological studies is with a study of God's call. Such a study at the beginning of an undergraduate or graduate theological degree could serve to inspire students and increase their hunger for greater biblical and theological learning. Students tend to be full of questions regarding God's call at the beginning of formal theological education, whether undergraduate or graduate.

Second, I want to provide a written resource about God's call that may be helpful to lay readers as well as to those called to the ministry. In church life, many persons other than clergy feel called to some form of non-ordained ministry or service. Many of the characteristics of God's call are similar for both groups.

Third, I want this book to be a ready resource for professors, pastors, ministers, and mentors to have available to give to persons seeking their wisdom and counsel relative to God's call. Many times I have wished I had such a volume at my fingertips to offer to inquiring persons. I hope this book will meet this need.

A theme of personal conviction will provide the foundation for this book. This conviction is that "it is worth a life" to answer God's call. This is true for persons called to vocational ministry and equally true for those called to ministries not requiring ordination. The call of God is not exclusive to clergy, as special as that call is. God's call can come to all, and it is worth a life to serve God, whether as an ordained servant or layperson.

Chapter One will seek to set forth many of the characteristics usually present in a call experience. There is no one uniform way God calls people into his service. People do, however, encounter similar experiences when God calls. This chapter will identify many of these features for readers to consider and reflect upon.

Chapter Two will present the call stories of five people in the Bible—Samuel, Jeremiah, Mary, Jesus, and Paul. As the readers know, so many more could be presented, and some others will be. Nevertheless, the call stories of these five persons present rich and strong lessons about God's call, lessons that persons seeking to understand God's call should not miss.

Chapter Three seeks to describe the various ways God calls. Recognizing them will give people a ready connection to understand their individual calling. In addition, few people come to an acceptance of God's call via a straight path. More times than not, crooked and winding paths are present along the journey. Great lessons can be learned from valuing the bends and turns of life's experiences that often result in answering a call from God.

Chapter Four will address two practical matters of living into a call from God. The first topic will be to show the connection between obeying a call from God and the surprising places God may lead one to serve. The second topic will focus on answering the most frequently asked question about God's call: "How can I be sure this calling is from God?"

Chapter Five will explore the important question of the relationship between call and ordination. Answering a call from God and offering oneself for ordination are two different matters. This chapter will offer helpful guidance relative to whether ordination should be pursued.

The journey of hearing and responding to God's call usually develops over time. To be sure, direct and dramatic calls from God occur spectacularly and suddenly. But for most, the call of God is an evolving process.

A helpful image for this journey is the idea of "lantern theology." This image suggests that the journey to find one's calling often occurs in "lighted steps" along the way. This book will help readers discover and follow these lighted steps. So grab your lantern and let the journey begin. Remember, it is worth a life to answer God's call!

CHAPTER ONE

Characteristics of God's Call

"People are spiritually starving in an age of plenty."
(Richard Rohr, *What the Mystics Know*)[1]

Serious readers of the Bible discover early that the God revealed in Scripture and made incarnate in Jesus Christ is a God who calls. Call is one of the distinctive features of God's character. God calls men and women to share with him in his divine mission in the world. This has been true since God created the world, and it remains true today. How thrilling it is to consider, and to experience, that the God who called the great prophets and leaders of the Bible is calling persons today. God is a God who calls. The Gospel of John states this truth well: *You did not choose me, but I chose you to go and bear fruit—fruit that will last* (15:16).

The subject of God's call is such a vast topic that one's thoughts tend to tumble over one another in contemplation of this divine reality. This chapter seeks to ignite the reader's thinking about God's call by highlighting characteristics frequently experienced in hearing and responding to a call from God. Persons answering God's call in today's world can discover what so many who have preceded them have found: It is worth a life to live out a call from God.

A Call Story to Launch Our Study

Let us consider a story that comes early in the Bible to begin our thinking relative to factors involved in hearing and responding to a call from God. The call of Abraham and Sarah beginning in Genesis 12 (actually Gen. 11:27-31) illustrates important features of God's call. The passage below describes Abram's call from God:

Now the Lord said to Abram, "Go from your country and your kindred and your father's house to the land that I will how you. I will make of you a great nation, and I will bless you, and make your name great, so that you will be a blessing. I will bless those who bless you, and the one who curses you I will curse; and in you all the families of the earth shall be blessed. (vv. 1-3)

The Old Testament begins the life story of Israel, the people of God. Abraham stands as the first of the patriarchs, sometimes called the founding fathers of Israel. God called Abraham, and he and his wife Sarah became the forebearers of a new covenant people.

A first lesson evident in the call story of Abram and Sarai (their names at this point in the narrative) is that calls from God do not occur in a vacuum. They come in historical contexts and in the midst of existing life situations. God calls in real time.

Abram and Sarai were dealing with a difficult issue near the time of their call (Gen. 11:30; 15:1-2). This issue was barrenness, a stressful problem for married couples. While coping with this problem, Abram and Sarai likely concluded that their blessings were still abundant in that they were being called to become pioneers of a new covenant people—such a large mission for God. This story illustrates that calls from God come in real time, while personal life situations are being lived out. This characteristic is always present in the call stories of the Bible.

Sometimes God's call comes when hard conditions are present, either personally or in the world. This same truth can be seen in the call of Moses. God called Moses to return to Egypt and to bring the Hebrew slaves out of bondage. Moses hesitated at first in obeying this call because there was a "price on his head" back in Egypt (Exod. 2:14-15). Similarly, the call of Samuel occurred at a time in Israel's history when "the word of the LORD was rare and visions were not widespread" (1 Sam. 3:1). Should your call experience occur at a hard time in your life or in the culture, do not dismiss or postpone your deliberations. As stated, God's calls happen in real historical and personal contexts.

A second lesson relative to God's call evident in Abram and Sarai's story was the difficulty they had in seeing the future. God's call to them to embark on this divine mission to become forebearers of a chosen people and to journey to an unfamiliar land was not without risk. As thrilling as a call experience can be, sometimes it can raise a lot of questions about one's future. Surely Abram and Sarai thought more than once, "Where will this call take us? What results will it bring?" Often in our call experiences we are eager to respond affirmatively to God, but questions about our future welfare give us pause. Abram and Sarai gave the correct responses when considering the uncertainty about their call: They obeyed, and God showed them the next steps to take. Confirmation of a call can come from taking action first, after which knowledge follows. This idea will be presented in a later chapter.

Striking in this call story is a third lesson. God can bless you and use you in ways you never imagined. A promise from God came to Abraham (called by this name at this point in the story) that he would become "a father of many nations" (Gen. 17:5). This same promise came to Sarah (her name now in the narrative), telling her that she would be the "mother of nations" (Gen. 17:16). Father? Mother? Surely Abraham and Sarah wondered if they had heard God correctly. To be parents was the prayer of their hearts. And as we now know, God fulfilled his promises to Abraham and Sarah in ways beyond their expectations. The same may happen for us as we follow and are obedient to God's call.

The promise of blessing extended beyond Abraham and Sarah. They would not only be blessed, but would become a blessing to others. This is always an important point when considering a call from God. It is always for the benefit of others.

Here, then, are some beginning lessons for those seeking to understand some of the components of a call from God. God's call comes in the context of real-life situations and can lead one toward a future not easily seen. God's call is always for the benefit of others. The right response to a call is obedience. Trust the lighted paths God gives at the moment. He will reveal the next steps. The great reward may be that he will use you in ways you never imagined. What other lessons can you find in the call story of Abraham and Sarah?

God's Call to All

This first story about the call of Abraham and Sarah introduces us to the dynamics a person might experience in responding to a call from God. Let us build on the insights of our opening story to consider additional features of God's call.

Christian believers have been taught through the ages that the highest call from God is one that comes to all—to believe in Jesus Christ as Lord and receive the gift of salvation. To be sure, this is true. To believe in Christ is a universal call from God that comes to all persons. All Christians are also called to be servants and to minister to others.

Accompanying this truth is another exciting aspect of God's call: It does not come just for those entering professional ministry. His call is far wider. It extends to persons of various ages, backgrounds, and spiritual gifts to render all types of ministries and services in the world. A call to be a scientist or an educator can be a call from God, just as a call to become a member of the clergy is. However, such a view does require discretion and discernment. There are professions which may not honor God or his divine purposes in the world. Nevertheless, it is true that God calls persons for ministry and service inside and outside the church. The challenge is to discern God's call for you.

Has there been a greater example of this truth in recent years than that of Pope Francis? Almost simultaneously with his selection as pope came his example and witness to the world of the basic calling of all Christians—to be disciples of Jesus. In the earliest days of his papacy, the world saw Pope Francis washing the feet of the poor, embracing persons considered untouchables, and announcing blessings upon "the least of these" (Matt. 25:40). His actions awakened a new awareness in all Christians of the basic call we all share—to love as Christ loves. The humility and obedience of Pope Francis have been a meaningful example to all, clergy and laity. Mark Labberton says it well:

> Since Pope Francis has long followed his call to follow Jesus, now as pope he is simply continuing to do the same. The shock is that despite being pope, Francis is living as a Christian.[2]

The Concept of Missional Calling

In recent years, a new concept has emerged in ecclesiastical life that enlarges some of our traditional understandings of calling. This new concept is termed "missional calling." Understanding and interpreting calling as missional is the direct result of transition and changes currently occurring in society and in church life.[3] A few traditions about church, in particular, are changing. Institutional loyalty is not as great today as in times past. Rather than excessive preoccupation with "getting people back into church," missional theology seeks to redirect attention to "what God is doing in the world." Rather than an overemphasis upon questions that point to a "direct" calling ("Do you want to be a pastor?"), a missional view of calling asks, "What do you want to do for God?"[4]

Thus, missional understandings of calling expand traditional views by seeking to cultivate a kingdom-of-God vision of service and not just a local church vision of ministry. Missional theology seeks for the church to engage in ministries that build the kingdom and not just local institutions. In simple terms, the church should focus more on ministry than attendance.

Understanding calling as missional invites persons to consider the difference their lives could make for God and the world. Examples of missional callings might be one or more of the following:

- Caring for children who are victims of war and violence;
- Ministering to disabled veterans;
- Providing counseling for troubled teenagers;
- Creating breakfast places for the homeless in one's city;
- Reaching younger, unchurched adults for Bible study and fellowship.

As you can see, missional callings tend to vary in kind and scope. A direct calling to a particular missional calling can happen. Missional callings can come from or lead to a kingdom vision of ministry and not just an institutional or denominational vision.

Doug Koskela, in his book *Calling and Clarity: Discovering What God Wants for Your Life*, makes the point that a missional calling can be a primary factor of one's calling during the younger or formative years.[5] My experience with students confirms this view. University students, early in their studies, have some general ideas about what they desire to do for others. Their responses to questions of career and calling often reflect indecisiveness, but most give responses more global in nature. "I want to help the poor" or "I want to serve underprivileged people" are typical responses. By the time students reach graduation and consider employment opportunities or graduate schools, their understanding of calling generally becomes more specific.

Koskela lists five features of missional calling that are helpful in understanding this concept:

- Missional calling generally aligns with your gifts.
- Missional calling generally involves something that you are passionate about and that gives you joy.

- Missional calling is usually discerned following significant time, prayer, and communal involvement.
- Missional calling can be lived out in many ways throughout a person's life, not just through career or work.
- The field or direction of a missional calling generally does not shift dramatically over a lifetime.[6]

Thus, missional understanding of calling is now an additional way to think about a calling. This concept draws on the needs one may see in the world or in people's lives, needs that urge one to respond. A missional understanding of calling does not replace direct callings from God to enter particular professions or to go to selected places for ministry. A missional approach to calling seeks to redirect attention from institutional maintenance of the church to serving God in the world. Perhaps a helpful way to bring together the traditional idea of a direct call with this newer concept of missional calling is to consider a word from Frederick Buechner. Buechner, the widely acclaimed American writer, theologian, and minister, offers this quote about calling: *God calls one to the place where your deep gladness and the world's deep hunger meet.*[7]

To unpack Buechner's words can provide insight into one's call. What do you love doing the most? Is your main love preaching, doing missions, or helping the needy? What do you feel the world needs the most? Is there insight for your calling at the intersection of what gives you deep joy and what the world needs?

Additional Influences That Shape God's Calls

As indicated earlier, God's calls do not happen in a vacuum or outside the context of one's life experiences. God's calls come in real time. This was illustrated in the opening discussion of the call to Abraham and Sarah, and in the call stories of all persons in the Bible.

Some additional characteristics present in call situations can influence both the hearing of and response to a call from God. These influences can be seen working in the background of an individual's life or can be prime movers in evoking a positive response to God's call. These characteristics, outlined below, are "general" in the sense that they may operate in different ways with different persons. Nevertheless, they can have significant impact upon how one interprets a call experience. As you read, consider the impact any or all of these factors have had or may be having on your interpretation of God's call to you.

1. *A sense of restlessness within one's spirit or life situation.*

A theme frequently heard in call testimonies is the idea of a previous sense of restlessness or unhappiness active in one's spirit or life situation. Such restlessness may have caused one to become more intentional about seeking God's call or God's will for one's life. To be sure, this is not always the case. But often this experience is reported.

Examples might include a university student unhappy in a chosen major, an older adult who knows he or she is in the wrong profession, or a second-career individual who is plagued with regret for not answering God's call when it came years earlier. Another source of restlessness could be the knowledge of sin in a person's life and the conviction that one needs to abandon a sinful lifestyle and turn to God. In general, individuals may respond to a call when they conclude that their current life paths or vocational identities are not fulfilling God's plan for them. Such restlessness can provide incentives to open one's heart and spirit to a serious search for God's will or call.

Have you ever experienced this sense of restlessness in your life? Did you discern a connection between this restlessness and the time being right to answer God's call, or to become more intentional about seeking God's will for your life?

2. *A "tug of the heart."*

Alice Cullinan, in her book *Sorting It Out: Discerning God's Call To Ministry*, speaks of the "tug of the heart" as she writes about God's call.[8] This image is insightful. There are conditions in the world and in people's lives that cry out for response and evoke a deep desire within us to help. To witness the suffering of children in a war-ravaged region, for example, can evoke a determination to do something to help them. The need to do something is tugging at our hearts.

Examples are many and varied. A young man or woman may answer a call to youth ministry out of a desire to see young people come to Christ. Another person may answer a call to work in inner-city ministries after witnessing the burden of those living in poverty. A young man may turn down acceptance to medical school because of a greater desire to preach the gospel and to witness salvation become a reality in the lives of others. Or a person may leave seminary to answer a call to serve as one who seeks to protect the environment.

What are some of the needs of the world and of people that "tug" at your heart? Can you make a connection between these needs and the call you are experiencing or have experienced? For practice, list some of the things that tug at your heart in the margins of this page.

3. *Affirmation from others.*

A third factor that sometimes awakens one to the possibility of being called is affirmations of "witnessed ministry or spiritual gifts" one receives from significant others. These affirmations suggest that others are impressed by the gifts and abilities of the person doing ministry. I do not speak here of formal confirmation procedures related to ministry, such as ordination or denominational licensure. Rather, I speak of the affirmations and encouraging responses you may receive from people who observe you doing ministry. A pastor may say to a young intern, "You have 'preacher' written all over you." Or church members, at various times and without collaboration, may say the same thing to a staff member: "You have the best heart for missions I have ever seen." Such affirmations can serve as both recognitions of spiritual gifts and indicators of a call from God.[9]

Affirmations not only come from others but also from experiences in ministry, disciplined prayer, and the convictions of the Holy Spirit. Examples might include a divinity student doing clinical pastoral education and declaring, "I never feel more at home than when I am in the hospital." Another person may say that her happiest moments are "when I am singing in worship or before audiences." Such self-evaluations may indicate a call to some kind of ministry and, along with the affirmations from others, are one of the ways God calls. Such positive and helpful words may provide an opening for the Holy Spirit to nudge one toward a new life direction.

These examples are not exhaustive but suggest the influences that may be working in the background of a call experience. Over and beyond these influences is the knowledge that the Holy Spirit is at work in our lives in amazing and mystical ways. But be alert. Sometimes the convicting word about a call from God and about the use of your spiritual gifts can come through other people.

A Theologian's Categories of God's Calls

H. Richard Niebuhr, an important 20th-century American theologian and ethicist, wrote about the ways human beings relate to God. His analysis of the elements of God's call remain helpful today and provide a good summary of many of the points made in this chapter. In *The Purpose of The Church and Its Ministry*, Niebuhr offers four basic elements of God's call:

- *The Call to be a Christian.* This is the "call to discipleship of Jesus Christ, to hearing and doing the word of God, and to repentance and faith."
- *The Secret Call.* This is the inner persuasion and call experienced when a person feels directly summoned or invited by God to take up the work of the ministry.
- *The Providential Call.* This is the invitation and summons to assume the work of ministry that is before you, where your talents match up with the necessary office and work that is needed. Divine guidance often comes in the form of affirmation and confirmation.
- *The Ecclesiastical Call.* This is the summons extended to a man or woman by some community or institution of the church to engage in the work of ministry related to that institution or community of faith. Example: One is called to serve in a local church as a pastor or staff minister.[10]

These categories of understanding God's call include many of the concepts discussed in this chapter. Particularly helpful are Niebuhr's descriptions of the ways to understand the different categories. A call may arise from seeing overwhelming needs and believing one's gifts can address those needs (the Providential Call). A call may come from an inner conviction that God is calling one to ministry (the Secret Call). A call to serve in a particular church or institution is yet another category of a call experience (the Ecclesiastical Call).

You may identify with more than one of these categories. You may have used different terms to describe them. These categories can be helpful in describing and labeling our call experiences. Do any of them stand out to you?

Call, Vocation, and Profession

In this chapter, a number of characteristics related to God's call have been introduced. Before we proceed, perhaps clarifying some common terms related to call may be helpful.

Theologically, call and vocation are best understood as one. The word "vocation" comes from the Latin word *vocare*, which means "to call." This word can also mean "to summon."[11] Since all are called to be Christians, it naturally follows that all Christians have the same vocation—to be a disciple of Jesus Christ. Our calling is our vocation.

A problem exists, however, with the term "vocation" in our culture. The idea that a vocation represents a calling has been largely replaced by a view that a vocation represents a career, or how one earns a living. Persons who view vocation in this way seldom connect it to the idea of calling. Instead, they understand it more in terms of finding a job, earning an income, and becoming self-supportive. Vocation is thus defined for many in economic rather than theological terms.

It may be helpful to think of vocation coming first and profession coming second. Vocation (calling) originates first and is followed by profession (service or ministry). Professions arise out of our calling. This is not to say that calling and profession cannot be the same, but it is to say that in terms of order, appropriate professions should arise out of our callings.

These distinctions are important because people spend a majority of their adult lives in some kind of employment. Missional calling rightly encourages all to glorify God in their daily work and experiences. We are exhorted by Jesus to be "the salt of earth and the light of the world" (Matt. 5:13-14) wherever we serve and live.

Direct callings from God do come, and lifelong professions can result from these callings. I have loved my profession, and I am grateful for all the joys I have experienced. Those called to other professions could voice the same testimony.

Scriptural Admonitions

When the time arrived for Jesus to begin his public ministry, he called twelve disciples to join him. As we know from the Gospel narratives, Jesus not only called these twelve but also equipped them for their roles in the mission. The Gospel of Mark describes the focus of the ministry of the disciples: *And he (Jesus) ordained twelve, that they should be with him, and that he might send them forth to preach, and to have power to heal sickness, and to cast out demons* (3:14-15).

Note the first requirement of a called disciple of Jesus: "to be with him" (Mark 3:14). This instruction is easy to miss. Before one goes out to preach or to minister to the needs of people, Jesus expects the called person to spend time with him. This is because Jesus put himself at the center of his teachings. He has more to give called persons than a body of content.

Jesus knew that eventually he would have to turn his work on earth over to disciples. Thus, it became essential that they understood the work as only he could make clear. Spending focused time with the Lord, then and now, is crucial for effective Christian leadership and is the first requirement of a called person.

What a helpful word this is for those who are called: Let our first priority be to live in holy conversation with the Father. Prayer, indeed, is the key; it is the engine that will grow this relationship. These sacred devotional times result in discovering divine guidance and empowerment for the tasks one is called to do. The first requirement, then, for a called disciple should not be lost on us: *Spend time with the Lord.* As a result of doing so, disciples are to then go, proclaim the good news, and care for others (Mark 3:14-15).

The Scriptures offer a second inspiring word for called persons as they are discerning and interpreting a call: *Live a holy life.* This verse is found in 1 Peter:

> Therefore prepare your minds for action; discipline yourselves; set all your hope on the grace that Jesus Christ will bring you when he is revealed. Like obedient children, do not be conformed to the desires that you formerly had in ignorance. Instead, as he who called you is holy, be holy yourselves in all your conduct; for it is written, 'You shall be holy, for I am holy.' (1:13-16)

Just as faith and conduct go together, so do calling and witness. The internal challenge—spend time with the Lord—is accompanied by the external challenge—live a holy and exemplary life.

This text reminds us that we have a high vocation to fulfill. An earlier teaching of Jesus comes quickly to mind: "From everyone to whom much has been given, much will be required" (Luke 12:48).

Hear the key ideas and applications from this passage in 1 Peter: Pull yourself together mentally, accept the challenge of hard theological thinking, straighten out any unholy patterns in your life, be steady and reasonable, and reflect Christ's holiness in all of your conduct.[12]

Here, then, are two excellent admonitions that help one to uderstand God's call: Spend time with the Lord in prayer, and live a holy life.

Subtract for Success

For fifteen years of my professional life, I served as dean of Campbell University Divinity School. At the beginning of each term, in August and January, I had the privilege of addressing the new students in the incoming classes. My message was the same to them each time and was titled "Subtract for Success."

Early in this message, I would make the bold statement that "the kingdom of God grows by subtraction." Seeing the quizzical looks on the students' faces, I would then move quickly to explain my point.

My message was that they could not add graduate theological education to their already busy lives without finding things to subtract from their schedules and commitments. They should not add graduate-level studies to overly busy schedules and expect to do well. Therefore, I challenged them to find things to subtract from their lives and schedules to make room for divinity studies and experiences. The response was always positive and immediate. Most did not leave that day without thinking of things they could subtract to create the potential for success in school.

The kingdom of God, to be sure, grows by addition. But it also grows by subtraction. As we eliminate things from our lives that deter our walking with God, more room develops for the Holy Spirit to work within us. Hear this message as you consider God's call: subtract for success.

God, then, is a God who calls. It is God's choice to call men and women to participate with him in the great work of Christian ministry. God may call likely and unlikely candidates for mission with him, whether to church-related vocations or to other types of missions and ministries. His call to persons comes in real time and in specific historical and personal contexts. God's call can be unmistakably clear at the outset of recognizing a call experience, or it may unfold gradually in a person's life.

Early indicators of a call experience may include the passions that reside in a person's life for God, for the work of the church, or for needed ministries in the world. Additional indicators can include a sense of restlessness with one's station in life, a previous feeling of being called, or encouragement and affirmation of others.

Ben Campbell Johnson gives a good description of how a call begins and is brought to fruition:

> The call to ministry exists first in the mind of God. It remains a mere possibility until the person and situation coalesce through the power of a call. God waits for the right moment and the right person. The call finds receptivity in the heart and soul of that right person, and new possibilities are awakened in the person's mind and heart.[13]

Questions for Discernment

1. What aspects of Abraham's and Sarah's call connect with the characteristics you are experiencing with your call?

2. Can you identify with any of Doug Koskela's five features of missional calling? Which one speaks the most to you?

3. Have you experienced "a sense of restlessness" or a "tug of the heart" in your life?

4. Where do you sense that your spiritual gifts and passions are leading you?

5. Are there things you need to subtract from your life to fulfill God's will?

Notes

[1]Richard Rohr, *What the Mystics Know* (New York: The Crossroads Publishing Company, 2015), 16.

[2]Mark Labberton, *Called: The Crisis and Promise of Following Jesus Today* (Westmont, IL: InterVarsity Press, 2014), 166.

[3]Terry R. Hamrick, *Leadership in Constant Change: Embracing a New Missional Reality* (Atlanta: Cooperative Baptist Fellowship, 2012), 8.

[4]Ibid., 17-18.

[5]Doug Koskela, *Calling and Clarity: Discovering What God Wants for Your Life* (Grand Rapids: Wm. B. Eerdmans Publishing Co., 2015), xiv.

[6]Ibid., 6-7.

[7]Frederick Buechner, *Wishful Thinking: A Seeker's ABC* (New York: Harper and Row, 1994), 95.

[8]Alice Cullinan, *Sorting It Out: Discerning God's Call to Ministry* (Valley Forge, PA: Judson Press, 1999), 23.

[9]Ibid.

[10]H. Richard Niebuhr, *The Purpose of the Church and Its Ministry* (New York: Harper and Row, 1956), 64.

[11]Dennis Campbell, *Who Will Go For Us? An Invitation to Ordained Ministry* (Nashville: Abingdon Press, 1994), 16.

[12]Elmer G. Homrighausen, "1 Peter," in *The Interpreters Bible*, ed. George Arthur Buttrick (New York: Abingdon Press, 1957), vol. 12, 100.

[13]Ben Campbell Johnson, *Hearing God's Call: Ways of Discernment for Clergy and Laity* (Grand Rapids: Wm. B. Eerdmans Publishing Co., 2003), 110.

CHAPTER TWO

Biblical Lessons of God's Call

Then I heard the voice of the Lord saying,
"Whom shall I send? And who will go for us?"
And I said, "Here am I. Send me!" (Isa. 6:8)

The biblical narratives present informative stories of God calling individuals, stories that can be helpful to us. These stories, rich and varied in context, contain valuable lessons for anyone seeking to understand God's call.

Ben Campbell Johnson, professor emeritus of Christian spirituality at Columbia Theological Seminary, makes an important point when he says, "God not only speaks directly through a text in scripture but always speaks in accordance with the teachings of scripture."[1] Thus, although the call stories of the Bible are as varied as the individuals being called, in each story God's character remains consistent.

John Calvin, the renowned theologian, emphasized this point in his writings. He highlighted the "inner testimony" of Scripture[2] and stressed that the words of Scripture have the most power when the Spirit of God moves to make them come alive in the reader's consciousness.[3] Thus, as we study the call stories in the Bible, the Holy Spirit may impart insights applicable to our lives, but these insights will be consistent with God's character and his calls through the ages.

In this chapter we will examine five biblical call stories, those of Samuel, Jeremiah, Mary, Jesus, and Paul. They are chosen from many other call stories that could be examined, such as those of Moses, Ezekiel, or Isaiah. The five stories selected highlight features that could be helpful in understanding God's call today. In a few cases, they raise issues about God's call that are not often addressed. As you read these stories, write in the margins your reflections and any potential implications for you. And, as John Calvin hoped for his readers, may the Spirit of God move upon the stories and upon you as you read and reflect upon them.

The Call of Samuel:
Preparing a New Leader for a New Day

God calls new leaders for new days. The call of Samuel illustrates this truth. Samuel would be called by God to exercise critical leadership for Israel in the midst of a challenging time. So special were the call and leadership of this man that the Gospel writers borrow the phrase describing Samuel to describe Jesus: *And he grew in stature and in favor with God and with men* (1 Sam. 2:26; Luke 2:52).

Samuel's call experience happened early in his life, as 1 Samuel 3:1-10 reports:

> Now the boy Samuel was ministering to the Lord under Eli. The word of the Lord was rare in those days; visions were not widespread. At that time Eli, whose eyesight had begun to grow dim so that he could not see, was lying down in his room; the lamp of God had not yet gone out, and Samuel was lying down in the temple of the Lord, where the ark of God was. Then the Lord called, "Samuel! Samuel!" and he said, "Here I am!" and ran to Eli, and said, "Here I am, for you called me." But he said, "I did not call; lie down again." So he went and lay down. The Lord called again, "Samuel!" Samuel got up and went to Eli, and said, "Here I am, for you called me." But he said, "I did not call, my son; lie down again." Now Samuel did not yet know the Lord, and the word of the Lord had not yet been revealed to him. The Lord called Samuel again, a third time. And he got up and went to Eli, and said, "Here I am, for you called me." Then Eli perceived that the Lord was calling the boy. Therefore Eli said to Samuel, "Go, lie down; and if he calls you, you shall say, 'Speak, Lord, for your servant is listening.'" So Samuel went and lay down in his place. Now the Lord came and stood there, calling as before, "Samuel! Samuel!" And Samuel said, "Speak, for your servant is listening."

Before discussing the important elements in Samuel's call, let us not miss one feature of the historical context of this passage. Samuel was called in a time when spiritual leaders were needed and people perceived that God's voice and work were not as vigorous as in times past. The text is candid: *In those days the word of the Lord was rare; there were no frequent visions* (1 Sam. 3:1).

As noted earlier in our discussion of Abraham's call, God's call comes in historical contexts, even personal ones, and Samuel's call certainly did. God's calls happen in the same way in our age. They may come in the midst of difficult personal issues or in challenging cultural times, or both. God calls leaders for such times.

Samuel's call story is special. He was born to a mother who longed for a son and promised to return him to the Lord once born. He spent his early life in the temple living near the ark of God and the priest Eli, and as an adult he led Israel at a critical time in its history. But there are still lessons to be learned from Samuel's call.

1.   *The importance of being in places where God's call can be heard.*

Samuel's call came to him in the temple during a time of service to Eli the priest. Readers should not rush by this fact. To be sure, God's call can come at any time and at any place. God is not limited in where and how he can speak. Nevertheless, there may be a relationship between hearing the call and being in a place where we are likely to be listening. God may be calling persons today whose spirits are not responsive. Could it be that these persons are in places where God's call is not expected and thus cannot be heard?

Fortunately, Samuel was in a place where God's voice could be heard. Remember the opening verse of Samuel's call story: "The word of the Lord was rare in those days" (1 Sam. 3:1). Was it rare because God was not speaking or because the people were not listening? An important lesson from Samuel's call is to seek those places and associates in your life where God's voice can be heard and acknowledged.

2.   *The importance and value of mentors.*

Samuel was also fortunate to have a significant and influential person in his life to give guidance as he sought to understand the voice he was hearing. The text clearly states that Eli, not Samuel, was the first to discern that the Lord was calling Samuel. This is an important part of the story. Eli had become blind (1 Sam. 3:2), yet he was the one to "see" that God was calling Samuel.

Mentors can play an important role in the call process. Callings can be nurtured and influenced by mentors who take an interest in our lives and offer guidance in our journeys. And do not forget a truth you already know: God's hand is often at work in our lives long before we recognize it. This was certainly true for Samuel. Sometimes we do not understand these shaping influences until we are much older. Mentors assist us in interpreting the spiritual movements in our lives that may have been developing over time.

The value of mentors has been evident in my life. A pastor and his wife, both now deceased, took an interest in me during my final year in high school. At the beginning of my senior year, this couple asked my parents for permission to take me on a visit to a church-related college they supported. Their purpose was to encourage me to make this school my college choice. Following high school graduation, I enrolled in and attended the college. Little did I know at the time that this campus would be where I would hear God's call to vocational ministry. I was in a place where God's call could be heard. Many of my professors became lifelong mentors. This campus would also be the place where I would meet my future wife, and we have been together now for more than four decades. How thankful I am for the mentors, like this wonderful couple, who God has used to guide me in the ways I could not foresee.[4]

Who have been the Elis in your life? Take a moment to give thanks to God for their influence on you. Are you ready to be an "Eli" to a young Samuel you know?

3.   *Do not miss in Samuel's story that, in due time, he took his place as a leader for Israel in the time and place God needed him.*

By the time Samuel reached adulthood, Israel was facing a crisis. The leadership of the judges was waning, and the forthcoming era of Israel's kings—Saul, David, and Solomon—had not yet arrived. Samuel was Israel's needed leader during this "in-between" time. The seams holding Israel together were strained. Good leaders were in short supply. Samuel stood in this gap. He kept the people's eyes on God and on the future. Not a perfect person himself nor a supporter of the emerging monarchy, Samuel nevertheless would anoint two of the next three kings of Israel. He fulfilled the calling heard that sacred night in the temple and became the leader God wanted and his people needed.

These, then, are some lessons we might learn from studying the call of Samuel. Do you see other lessons in this story? Dedicated leaders are always needed for God's work. Could you be one of them?

The Call of Jeremiah: God's Prophet for a Crisis Era

In his painting of Jeremiah in the Sistine Chapel in Rome, Michelangelo depicted the prophet as a person of great strength whose right shoulder is weighed down by a heavy burden. As one looks past Jeremiah's stooped shoulder, one sees the figure of a seemingly tragic woman. She appears to be in deep despair. Behind the left shoulder of the prophet, a different figure can be seen. It is a young man with a bright glow on his face.[5]

With these contrasting images of burden and hope, Michelangelo captured the dual emphases of the prophet Jeremiah's preaching career. On the one hand, there was his preaching of judgment that God would bring upon an unrepentant people. On the other hand, there was the hope Jeremiah held out for the people of Judah if they would live in faithfulness and obedience to God.

God's call to Jeremiah came during a volatile period in the history of Judah. Both world conditions and domestic crises were factors surrounding Jeremiah's call. His ministry spanned the reigns of five kings of Judah (c. 640-587 BCE), with King Josiah being the most notable of the five. Internationally, three world powers—Assyria to the north, Egypt to the south, and Babylon to the east—were threats to Judah's security. Ironically, Jeremiah lived through one of the most significant periods of revival in Judah's history: the reforms of King Josiah. It was during this period that the long lost book of Deuteronomy was discovered by workers repairing a damaged area in the temple. As one author has noted, "This discovery allowed the Israelites to stand before Sinai again."[6]

An early supporter of Josiah's reforms, Jeremiah would later lose faith in the results of these changes. He came to believe that the people were putting their hopes in the rituals of life and religion rather than in revering the living God. He called on Judah to repent, to renew her vows to the God who had called her to be a covenant people, and to live in faithful obedience.

Over time, the external threat posed by Babylon would overcome Judah. Jeremiah would witness the sieges of the Babylonians on Jerusalem in 597 BCE and then again in 587 BCE. He saw his countrymen carried away against their wills into exile in Babylon. Jeremiah himself lived in exile in Egypt, never returning to his homeland.

During these final years of decline in Judah before the exile, Jeremiah preached an unpopular message. He believed Judah should have learned from the fate of the northern kingdom of Israel, which had already fallen because of its lack of repentance and infidelity to God's covenant. From this example, Jeremiah thought Judah should have known better. But Jeremiah came to see the conquest by the Babylonians as judgment on the people for their sins. The people of Judah never came to repentance, but Babylonian aggressors did come. Jeremiah took no joy in this judgment. He anguished for his people. The exile period came (587-538 BCE), and during this time Jeremiah would find a new message, one of hope and renewal for his people. His declaration of a "new covenant" (Jer. 31:27-34) formed the heart of his message to the people living in exile.

Jeremiah was a towering figure in his day. He was a prophet who bore grievous burdens, who witnessed a great national revival, who lived through plummeting spiritual declines, and who bore the burden of preaching to a largely unresponsive people. But let us now focus more intently on factors connected to his call to ministry. From Jeremiah 1:4-10, this is what we learn about God's call to his prophet:

> Now the word of the LORD came to me saying, "Before I formed you in the womb I knew you, and before you were born I consecrated you; I appointed you a prophet to the nations."
>
> Then I said, "Ah Lord God! Truly I do not know how to speak, for I am only a boy." But the LORD said to me, "Do not say, 'I am only a boy'; for you shall go to all to whom I send you, and you shall speak whatever I command you. Do not be afraid of them, for I am with you to deliver you, says the LORD."
>
> Then the LORD put out his hand and touched my mouth; and the LORD said to me, "Now I have put my words in your mouth. See, today I appoint you over nations and over kingdoms, to pluck up and to pull down, to destroy and to overthrow, and to build and to plant."

Because his father was a priest, Jeremiah was nurtured in a godly home. Possible interpretations of Jeremiah's name are "Yahweh hurls" or "Yahweh shoots."[7] Could it be that Jeremiah's parents sensed a destiny for their son to be called and "hurled" or "flung" by God into the role of a prophet to meet the spiritual needs of his culture? Jeremiah would later come to understand that God had consecrated and commissioned him before he was born (Jer. 1:5). Further, Jeremiah believed that he was called to be a "prophet to the nations" (Jer. 1:5). Unlike Isaiah, who volunteered for his mission (Isa. 6:8), Jeremiah believed that his call had happened before he was born.

Here is an extraordinary example of hearing and responding to God's call. Jeremiah discovered a destiny for his life. The meaning of his name—Yahweh hurls—may have been an indicator of his destiny. God had a purpose for him. Though initially reluctant to accept this destiny (Jer. 1:6-8), Jeremiah ultimately obeyed. In letting go of his own plans and accepting God's push, or call, Jeremiah fulfilled his destiny in a way he could never have foreseen and in a way that served God and his people.

Additional Lessons from Jeremiah's Call

Jeremiah's call is a profitable one to study. His conviction that he was called before he was born and that "God had shaped him" (Jer. 1:5) contrasts with many other biblical calls where persons are called later in life. What are some additional lessons about call that might be learned from Jeremiah's life and ministry?

1. *It all starts with God.*

As we have seen, God is the caller. God was planning for Jeremiah to be his messenger before Jeremiah knew it himself. God promised to Jeremiah his "word and words" (Jer. 1:4, 9). God's presence and his word were actively energizing Jeremiah long before the prophet understood what all this meant.

Jeremiah's call reminds us it all starts with God. In Jeremiah's call experience, note that there is no overwhelming consciousness of sin that needs to be recognized and dealt with, as in Isaiah's call (Isa. 6:5). The call experience starts with God and unfolds in Jeremiah's life. Jeremiah did what God asked him to do, and God kept his promise to be with Jeremiah (Jer. 1:18). The word of God to the young Jeremiah seeking to understand God's will for his life offers encouragement to others experiencing a call:

But you, gird up your loins (get yourself ready); stand up and tell them everything that I command you. Do not break down before them, or I will break you before them. And I for my part have made you today a fortified city, an iron pillar, and a bronze wall, against the whole land…for I am with you, says the Lord, to deliver you. (Jer. 1:17-19)

2. *Resistance to the call.*

Some who hear or feel God's call may attempt to resist it. Some called persons speak of fighting the call or running from it. Others say that they did not want to surrender to the call. Such resistance appears to be common in call stories. In the Bible, we read of resistance to the call in the experiences of Moses, Gideon, Isaiah, and Jonah, to name a few. Jeremiah's first concern about his calling was his age; he was young at the time of his call. There are many reasons to resist a call. Among them might be a sense of personal inadequacy, the fear that the challenge may be too difficult, anxiety about unanswered questions, or a mistake-filled past that could affect one's credibility or effectiveness. Sometimes resistance to what feels like God's call is realistic, and the issues involved should not be ignored.

But balanced against the reasons for resistance to God's call are God's reassuring promises and presence. This truth is seen in the many call stories in the Bible. God assures the individuals being called that he will be with them, empower them, and equip them for the work they are being asked to do. There is no reason to believe God will not do the same for us.

3. *Jeremiah was called for his times. We are called for ours.*

Demonstrated over and over again in the biblical call narratives is the truth that God's call happens in historical contexts. Like the other prophets before him, Jeremiah was called to minister during a difficult period. Overall, it could be said that he preached his entire career to a largely unresponsive people. His pleas for individual and national repentance rubbed like sandpaper across the culture of his day and time.

Occasionally someone today may say that we need to be "the New Testament church." Not really. While we may incorporate some patterns and practices from New Testament times into our ministry activities, the truth is that we are called to be the church in our time. We must strive to be the church and the ministers God needs now. Jeremiah was called for his day and time. We are called for ours.

4. *Our ministries will have short-term and long-term goals.*

Jeremiah's call to preach had immediate commissions from God. He was called "to uproot and tear down, to destroy and to overthrow" (Jer. 1:10). But Jeremiah's ministry would also have some long-term goals. He would be commissioned "to build and to plant" (Jer. 1:10).

We should remember that the Old Testament prophets were not without hope. It is a myth to think they were. Judgment, the prophets preached, is real. But what is also real is hope in God for the future and the new life that can come. In Jeremiah's case, he was given a new message to preach during the exile. This new message featured specific advice for the Israelites' living conditions (Jer. 29:4-14 is one example), but it also included hopeful prophecies for the future (Jer. 31:31-34). Our ministries must also meet the challenges to address immediate needs while looking ahead to lead God's people in the future.

Jeremiah's call and his subsequent ministry illustrate many lessons about hearing and responding to a call from God. Although Jeremiah had a unique call experience, he (like many of us) was called to minister in a difficult time. He preached and labored against overwhelming odds. He experienced success and failures as he responded to the challenge of ministering to his people in exile.

Whether one judges Jeremiah's ministry to be a success or failure, or a mixture of the two, he demonstrated faithfulness to his call.

The Call of Mary: God Calls a Woman

The Advent stories in the Bible are full of incidents in which God speaks through the Holy Spirit to his servants. In these stories, God speaks to Zechariah and Elizabeth, to Joseph and Mary, and to the wise men and the shepherds, to name a few. Through the evangelist John we hear proclaimed the heart of all the Advent proclamations: *The Word became flesh and dwelt among us. We have seen his glory, the glory of the one and only Son who came from the Father, full of grace and truth* (1:14).

Located behind this grand proclamation is a beautiful and inspiring call story of an individual hearing and responding to a call. It is the story of Mary, called to bring the Son of God to us so that we might proclaim him to the world. The Gospel of Luke tells the story:

> In the sixth month the angel Gabriel was sent by God to a town in Galilee called Nazareth, to a virgin engaged to a man whose name was Joseph, of the house of David. The virgin's name was Mary. And he came to her and said, "Greetings, favored one! The Lord is with you." But she was much perplexed by his words and pondered what sort of greeting this might be. The angel said to her, "Do not be afraid, Mary, for you have found favor with God. And now, you will conceive in your womb and bear a son, and you will name him Jesus. He will be great, and will be called the Son of the Most High, and the Lord God will give to him the throne of his ancestor David. He will reign over the house of Jacob forever, and of his kingdom there will be no end." Mary said to the angel, "How can this be, since I am a virgin?" The angel said to her, "The Holy Spirit will come upon you, and the power of the Most High will overshadow you; therefore the child to be born will be holy; he will be called Son of God. And now, your relative Elizabeth in her old age has also conceived a son; and this is the sixth month for her who was said to be barren. For nothing will be impossible with God." Then Mary said, "Here am I, the servant of the Lord; let it be with me according to your word." Then the angel departed from her. (1:26-38)

Gabriel's startling announcement bewildered Mary at first. Her feelings of confusion and inadequacy quickly surfaced. According to the text, she was actually afraid and felt inadequate to fulfill this request. When God first calls, it is not uncommon to feel inadequate.

After a while, Mary responded with questions of her own. Here, she teaches us a valuable lesson about call: It is perfectly acceptable to ask questions. What Mary needed was more information. Hear some of her questions: "What kind of greeting is this? How can all of this happen—I have no husband?" (Luke 1:29). What Gabriel was asking seemed impossible to Mary. She needed some issues to be clarified.

Gabriel welcomed Mary's questions, and God welcomes ours. Gabriel responded with words of assurance of God's presence and power. "With God," says the angel, "nothing is ever impossible" (Luke 1:37). As stated earlier, this feature of divine reassurance and presence seems to be present in every biblical situation where resistance to or reluctance about a call appears.

Note the next development in the story. Having asked her questions and received responses from the angel, Mary embraces her call. "I am the Lord's servant," she declares. "May it be to me as you have said" (Luke 1:38). Moffatt's translation of this verse states Mary's response even more powerfully: "I am here to serve the Lord" (Luke 1:38, Moffatt). Ben Campbell Johnson states that this response from Mary may be the purest expression of obedience in the New Testament.[8]

As with Abraham, Jeremiah, and Samuel, Mary's call came to her in an unusual and difficult context. She would be a young, unmarried pregnant girl in a culture where her pregnancy could have created problems, even scandal. Nevertheless, Mary said yes to God's call. She would give birth to the Son of God.

Mary's call experience teaches us that it is acceptable to ask questions and seek more information when a call is experienced. Consider some other lessons Mary's call teaches:

1. *Mary placed herself at God's disposal.*

God came to Mary (by means of the angel Gabriel) with a sacred mission. Once she understood the mission, she responded with readiness to serve the Lord. Let us remember that one of the greatest gifts we can give to God is to be a willing channel of his grace. Mary received grace and, in turn, became a vessel of grace.

Don't miss another element of calling we have discussed: confirmation. Mary follows up her encounter with Gabriel with a visit to her cousin Elizabeth. Like Mary, Elizabeth had also experienced a miraculous conception. Her son would be John the Baptist. Mary's visit and conversations with Elizabeth brought confirmation to Mary of the truth and wonder of Gabriel's announcement to her (Luke 1:36; 39-45).

2. *A song rises from Mary's heart to celebrate her call (Luke 1:46-55).*

Mary's song of praise to God, the Magnificat, expresses her praise and thanksgiving in celebration of her faith and her call. The words of her song reflect the thoughts and praises in her heart for what God is about to do through her. As we live out our callings, may our faithfulness and dedication lead to similar praise to God.

3.   *God did not ask Mary to do his part of the work. He asked her to do only her part.*

God needs our help for his will to be done, but God does not ask us to do his part. This is something servants of God forget at times. God has not called us to do his part of the work, only ours. Because of Mary's faith and obedience, God could depend on her. A good commitment to make relative to your call is pledging to God that he can depend on you for the work he has called you to do.

What a beautiful picture of God's call. Mary's commitment to God was not just for the moment but was a lifelong commitment. She was present at the beginning of the life of Jesus, and she was present at the end (John 19:25-29). What a portrait of faithfulness to the Lord.

The Call of Jesus: Savior for the World

Must I not be about my Father's business? (Luke 2:49)

A Carpenter Shop Story

The Gospel of John concludes with a global statement about the activities and ministries of Jesus: *But there are also many other things that Jesus did; if every one of them were written down, I suppose that the world itself could not contain the books that would be written* (21:25).

Surely one of these stories "not written down," or something like it, happened in a carpenter shop in Nazareth about the time Jesus was approaching age 30. At the right time, Jesus walked out of the carpenter shop and made his way to the Jordan River to be baptized by John and begin his ministry (Mark 1:9-11).

Imagine this scene with me. I can picture Jesus as a young man working in a carpenter shop in Nazareth, fitting into village life in a competent and exemplary manner. Apparently, as a faithful son, Jesus had kept Joseph's carpenter business operating. No one knows if Joseph had died by this time, but it is commonly assumed that he had. Speculation would suggest that during these years Jesus assisted Mary with the raising of his siblings and perhaps with financial support from his work as a carpenter. Later in his life, Jesus will be referred to at times as "the carpenter from Nazareth" (Matt. 13:55; Mark 6:3).

At some point, the following "invisible" scene, or something like it, must have happened. Jesus closed up the carpenter shop. What made him do so? When, indeed, did he see more in the wood than the shavings curling up from the plane? What made him place his carpenter's apron on the workbench, never to return? Surely there is no answer other than that the time had arrived for Jesus to fulfill God's calling on his life. Jesus then made his way to the Jordan River to be baptized by John the Baptist and to begin his public ministry.

When we are called, God sometimes asks us to leave our "carpenter shops" to respond to his summons. Where is your "carpenter shop?" How does this image fit into your story of hearing and responding to God's call?

Our carpenter shops are not to be forgotten once we leave them. Quite the contrary; much of what we learn in such places informs the ministries we render. To confirm this point, note the many times in the ministry of Jesus when he makes use of carpentry or building images. Jesus tells Peter that he will be "the rock upon which I will build my church" (Matt. 16:18). In addition, the parables of Jesus frequently include building themes. A few that illustrate this point would be the parables of The Wise and Foolish Builders (Matt. 7:24-29; Luke 6:46-49); the Parable of the Rich Fool (Luke 12:13-21); and the Parable of the Tenants (Matt. 21:33-44). In this last parable, Jesus said, "The stone the builders rejected has become the capstone" (Matt. 21:42). The apostle Paul will pick up on this saying at a later time when he describes Jesus as "the chief cornerstone of the household of God" (Eph. 2:19-22). Carpenter shop lessons were with Jesus throughout his ministry. What skills we have already developed may shape how we are called to serve.

Additional Lessons from the Call of Jesus

1. *Jesus was an inner-directed person.*

Elizabeth O'Connor, in her book *Cry Pain, Cry Hope: Thresholds of Purpose*, wrote that to hear the voice of God, one has to be "in a state of receptivity and attention with one's ear turned inward."[9] This was her way of saying that inner-directed persons are in the best positions to hear the impulses of a call.

Jesus was certainly an inner-directed person. His deep prayer life and closeness to God enhanced his attention to the directions God would give him for his ministry. Frequently, we read in the Gospels that Jesus would depart from places filled with crowds to follow the impulse of the Holy Spirit to carry his message to a new region. (Mark 1:35-39 is one example.)

Answering a call from God is different than finding a job. Other considerations besides salary, benefits, and career take priority when one responds to a call. These include the feeling of being summoned, the potential development of one's spiritual gifts, and the opportunities to serve others.

I have frequently asked divinity students, especially in early morning sections, "What motivated you to be here today? Was it the stock market report from yesterday or the promise of a high salary?" Of course, I knew these were not their motivations. They were there to receive the preparation needed to fulfill the work God had called them to do.

Being an inner-directed person may make it easier to stay on task in service to God. Jesus had this characteristic, and it served him well.

2.   *With Jesus, we learn that heeding a call is often bound up with economic risk.*

One topic seldom discussed relative to a call is the relationship between call and finances.[10] Responding affirmatively to a call from God does carry financial implications. This aspect of God's call should not be ignored in helping students and laypersons process their feelings about the calls they are experiencing. Financial concerns tend to be *a* factor and not *the* factor in how one responds to a call.

The conflict between answering a call from God and accepting the financial implications generally surface quickly. The idea of answering a call often does not look prudent to those looking on. An old comment is that "few have heard a call from God that everyone in the family understood and appreciated" (source unknown). And this is likely true far more often than not.

The ministry of Jesus illustrates this point. If, indeed, Jesus once managed a financially stable carpenter shop, it is ironic that he would later say that "the Son of Man has nowhere to lay his head" (Matt. 8:20; Luke 9:58). Clearly, Jesus experienced some downward mobility upon giving up income from a carpentry business to become an itinerant teacher and preacher.

Persons answering a call from God today often receive quizzical looks. In particular, second-career persons answering a call to ministry experience this reaction from people. Other people can hardly believe that the called person would sacrifice income and job security. It is certainly true that to begin theological education at a nontraditional age or to make a career change to undertake ministry activities can result in reduced income. While there are no guarantees, most who answer a call generally achieve financial equilibrium, although perhaps not to the level they had before. But many reach an equilibrium of personal satisfaction and financial security. And it is not uncommon to hear testimonies of the miracle and adequacy of God's provision from those who have made financial sacrifices to follow a call. Financial sacrifices are real, but God's provisions are also real.

3. *The call of Jesus teaches that responding to a call from God begins a new journey.*

When one answers a call to ministry or service for God, a journey is about to begin. For some, the journey is geographical: Abraham and Jonah were called to go to new places. But these journeys can also be inward, as the person who is called travels to new insights or deeper understanding by studying with a teacher or mentor.

People who feel they have been called would be wise to embrace the journey before them with open minds and committed hearts. They will learn much along the way, far more good than bad. These lessons will bless them for a lifetime.

The Call of Paul: God's Chosen Messenger for the Mission to the Gentiles

The man we meet early in the Book of Acts named Saul of Tarsus is destined to have a dramatic encounter with the risen Christ. As we know, Saul's conversion experience happened on the road to Damascus (Acts 9:1-9). His conversion, and his subsequent call to undertake a mission to the Gentiles, is one of the most famous call episodes in the Bible.

Interestingly, the call of Saul actually includes another call story—that of Ananias, a layman. Ananias was called by God to assist Saul in understanding his call, and to serve as a guide to Saul in the days following his conversion.

Although hesitant at first to befriend Saul, Ananias put aside his doubts and followed God's instructions.

The story of Ananias' role in Saul's conversion is exciting:

> But Ananias answered, "Lord, I have heard from many about this man, how much evil he has done to your saints in Jerusalem; and here he has authority from the chief priests to bind all who invoke your name." But the Lord said to him, "Go, for he is an instrument whom I have chosen to bring my name before Gentiles and kings and before the people of Israel; I myself will show him how much he must suffer for the sake of my name." So Ananias went and entered the house. He laid his hands on Saul and said, "Brother Saul, the Lord Jesus, who appeared to you on your way here, has sent me so that you may regain your sight and be filled with the Holy Spirit." And immediately something like scales fell from his eyes, and his sight was restored. Then he got up and was baptized, and after taking some food, he regained his strength. (Acts 9:13-18)

Note that there is no hint in the text that God was angry with Ananias for at first resisting God's instructions. Somehow Ananias found the faith and strength to complete the mission assigned to him. I wonder if Ananias ultimately took pride in having helped launch Paul's ministry.

There is more to Paul's being called than his loss of sight on the road to Damascus. Although Paul had been blind in his zealous persecution of early Christians, God was clear-sighted, seeing in Paul a man with strengths and gifts that could make him an effective witness to spread the good news of the Christ's sacrificial death and the salvation offered to all who believe. I would like to highlight four aspects of Paul's experience and preparation that fitted him for what he was called to do. Recognizing how Paul's strengths and experiences were used by God could be helpful to those considering a call today.

1. *Before becoming a missionary, Paul works as an ordinary laborer and clarifies what he believes by witnessing to and listening to others.*

> After this Paul left Athens and went to Corinth. There he found a Jew named Aquila, a native of Pontus, who had recently come from Italy with his wife Priscilla, because Claudius had ordered all Jews to

leave Rome. Paul went to see them, and, because he was of the same trade, he stayed with them, and they worked together—by trade they were tentmakers. Every Sabbath he would argue in the synagogue and would try to convince Jews and Greeks. (Acts 18:1-4)

Here, we learn of Paul's secular vocation. He was a tentmaker, a trade which allowed him quick identification with other tentmakers like Priscilla and Aquila. In this secular vocation Paul gained more than the friendship of fellow tentmakers. In today's vernacular, Paul learned what it is like "to work for the public." Working in public vocations teaches one a lot about people— their longings, their hurts, and their spiritual needs. This experience would be invaluable to Paul in his ministry.

In responding to God's call today, those who have already worked with or served the public are likely to have better insights into people and their needs. This real-world experience is a great asset. Those entering the ministry as a second career should never look upon their earlier years and careers as wasted time. Their experiences can be useful preparation for ministry and service. Perhaps one benefit of secular work experience is the insight one develops into the spiritual needs of people. It is intriguing to remember that the man God called to lead the mission to the Gentiles had to make a radical change in his own life. He was not a professional cleric but a layperson who had "worked for the public."

2. *Paul proudly declares that he studied under the great teachers of his day.*

"Brothers and fathers, listen to the defense that I now make before you." When they heard him addressing them in Hebrew, they became even more quiet. Then he said: "I am a Jew, born in Tarsus in Cilicia, but brought up in this city at the feet of Gamaliel, educated strictly according to our ancestral law, being zealous for God, just as all of you are today. (Acts 22:1-3)

In this passage, we see a positive correlation between calling and education. Paul expressed gratitude for the education he had received under a great teacher of his day, Gamaliel. Ben Campbell Johnson points out that "even though Paul learned a lot from Gamaliel, he still did not know enough about Christ to be a spokesperson for him."[11] Perhaps this was one reason for Paul's three years in Arabia (Gal. 1:17-18) or for the long delay before he began the missionary journeys. And Paul is clearly proud of the education he received from Gamaliel.

The relationship between calling and education has not always been fully appreciated, especially among Baptists. This undervaluing of education has been true for other denominations and religious groups as well.

George W. Paschal, in his *History of North Carolina Baptists*, cites a particular case of dissension on this issue that surfaced in a meeting of ministers in northeastern North Carolina in the late 1700s. After hearing vigorous arguments opposing education for clergy, a minister named Martin Ross (1762-1828) argued for "improvement in ministry," which included education for clergy. Paschal includes some of Ross' reasoning:

> Before we conclude, we beg leave to say a word to the Ministers of Christ among you, both old and young. 'Tis the great work of a minister to teach others, but particularly to teach the way of the Lord; and Ministers should be well instructed themselves in the way of the Lord. You are to feed the flock with knowledge and understanding. It is therefore necessary to be blessed with knowledge and understanding. Many have said, 'The Spirit of God needs none of man's learning.' With much greater truth it may be said 'The Spirit of God needs none of man's ignorance.' Noise and rant may set the world a gazing, but it is divine truth that turns souls to God.[12]

As mentioned, there have been mixed reactions to the idea of education as a requirement for effective ministry. This has been true among Baptists since their beginnings in England in the seventeenth century. The debate has usually focused on the relationship between using the best of one's intelligence or depending on the Holy Spirit to give you all you need to say or do. These were seen as opposites. A more wholesome view is to see them working together in the life of the minister and the believer. Persons called to ministry today should seek to follow the admonition of Jesus "to love God with all of your mind as well as your heart" (Mark 12:30).

In reflecting on Paul's appreciation for his education, there is one part of his story that might make us uncomfortable. We know that, for a season, Paul misused the good education he received. Before his conversion on the road to Damascus (Acts 9:1-3), he vigorously persecuted the Lord's disciples and believers. But we also know that Paul was nonetheless called by God and would eventually find his true path in ministry as one of the Lord's apostles.

Whether you are called to be a member of the clergy or a devoted layperson, strive to be a good steward of the education that you have received. The Bible offers a wealth of knowledge and truth—a treasure to be explored, taught, preached about, and lived out. Become someone who enjoys the rewards of study and learning. Cultivate a desire to preach and teach the Scriptures with accuracy. The fruits of your learning will then be used to bless others. Remember that you cannot preach or teach what you do not know.

3. *Paul quotes, without apology, from some of the Gentile philosophies of his day.*
    In Paul's famous sermon in Athens, he demonstrates his ability to defend the Christian faith and his ministry. In this passage, he is recognized as the first Christian philosopher to use Stoic and Jewish arguments:

> While Paul was waiting for them in Athens, he was deeply distressed to see that the city was full of idols. So he argued in the synagogue with the Jews and the devout persons, and also in the marketplace every day with those who happened to be there. Also some Epicurean and Stoic philosophers debated with him. Some said, "What does this babbler want to say?" Others said, "He seems to be proclaiming foreign divinities."

> So they took him and brought him to the Areopagus and asked him, "May we know what this new teaching is that you are presenting? It sounds rather strange to us, so we would like to know what it means."

> Then Paul stood in front of the Areopagus and said, "Athenians, I see how extremely religious you are in every way. For as I went through the city and looked carefully at the objects of your worship, I found among them an altar with the inscription, 'To an unknown god.' What therefore you worship as unknown, this I proclaim to you. The God who made the world and everything in it, he who is Lord of heaven and earth, does not live in shrines made by human hands, nor is he served by human hands, as though he needed anything, since he himself gives to all mortals life and breath and all things.

From one ancestor he made all nations to inhabit the whole earth, and he allotted the times of their existence and the boundaries of the places where they would live, so that they would search for God and perhaps grope for him and find him—though indeed he is not far from each one of us. For 'In him we live and move and have our being'; as even some of your own poets have said, 'For we too are his offspring.' Since we are God's offspring, we ought not to think that the deity is like gold, or silver, or stone, an image formed by the art and imagination of mortals. While God has overlooked the times of human ignorance, now he commands all people everywhere to repent. (Acts 17:16-18a, 19-20, 22-30)

This passage illustrates Paul's knowledge of some of the creeds and philosophies of his time and place. Stated simply, he had an awareness of "what was out there." Understanding trends in the culture helped Paul speak intelligently about them and present his convictions of faith more vigorously. As we serve God in our context, we should know "what is out there." This is a great lesson for us.

4. *Paul gives first place in his ministry to proclaiming the knowledge of God he now possesses.*

For the message about the cross is foolishness to those who are perishing, but to us who are being saved it is the power of God. Where is the one who is wise? Where is the scribe? Where is the debater of this age? Has not God made foolish the wisdom of the world? For Jews demand signs and Greeks desire wisdom, but we proclaim Christ crucified, a stumbling block to Jews and foolishness to Gentiles, but to those who are the called, both Jews and Greeks, Christ is the power of God and the wisdom of God. For God's foolishness is wiser than human wisdom, and God's weakness is stronger than human strength. (1 Cor. 1:18, 20, 22-25)

What a theological journey Paul has traveled! He gives testimony that he has come to believe that the knowledge he now possesses regarding God's work in Jesus Christ is his supreme intellectual possession. The key to the knowledge of God, says Paul, comes through learning about Jesus Christ and his sacrificial death on a cross. Thus, Paul gives this conviction first place in his ministry. He will not grow weary of preaching "Christ and Christ crucified." Paul wants all to know about God's work in Jesus.

Raymond Bryan Brown, late academic dean and Professor of New Testament at Southern and Southeastern seminaries, once said the following in a chapel address: "Knowledge of God is born out of service to God. We know God not when we stand outside his will and study him but when we stand within his will and serve him."[13]

What an insight. Knowledge about God and service for him go hand in hand. Let us give these truths about God first place in our lives, as Paul sought to do.

Questions for Discernment

1. Where, in your deliberations about God's call, do you connect with and relate to some of the characteristics seen in the call of Samuel?

2. Are there elements in Jeremiah's call and ministry that you have found true in your life? Can you elaborate on them?

3. How does the "carpenter shop" image presented in the call of Jesus speak to you?

4. What have your previous life experiences taught you about people and their spiritual needs? How has "working for the public" and/or "living a while" contributed to the ministry goals you seek?

Notes

[1] Ben Campbell Johnson, *Hearing God's Call*, 37.

[2] Ibid.

[3] Ibid.

[4] I wish to state the names of Dr. and Mrs. James R. Bruce (Helen) of Inman, S.C. I shall forever be grateful for the impact of their lives on me.

[5] Michelangelo, *Jeremiah*, 1509-10, Sistine Chapel, Rome.

[6] Roy L. Honeycutt, *Jeremiah: Witness Under Pressure* (Nashville: Convention Press, 1981), 5.

[7] James Leo Green, "Jeremiah," in *The Broadman Bible Commentary*, edited by Clifton J. Allen (Nashville: Broadman Press, 1971), vol. 6, 1.

[8] Ben Campbell Johnson, *Hearing God's Call*, 174.

[9] Elizabeth O'Connor, *Cry Pain, Cry Hope: Thresholds to Purpose* (Waco: Word Books, 1987), 81.

[10] Ibid., 82.

[11] Johnson, *Hearing God's Call*, 121.

[12] George W. Paschal, *History of North Carolina Baptists* (Raleigh: Baptist State Convention of NC, 1955), vol. II, 519-521.

[13] Richard A. Spencer, editor, *The Fire of Truth: Sermons by Raymond Bryan Brown* (Nashville: Broadman Press, 1982), 53.

CHAPTER THREE

The Ways God Calls

*But I will stay in Ephesus until Pentecost, for a wide door for effective work
has opened to me, and there are many adversaries.* (1 Cor. 16:8-9)

At times readers of the Bible miss some spiritual treasures in God's word
that are hiding in plain sight. This is especially true, I think, with passages
found in the last chapters of the books in the Bible. It seems easy, for some
reason, to not read these chapters and verses as carefully as one might read
previous chapters.

An excellent Scripture passage that relates to hearing and responding to
God's call is found in the last chapter of 1 Corinthians. In verses 8-9, Paul is
sharing his travel plans with the believers in Corinth and his hope to return to
the area as soon as possible. He informs them that he cannot return to the area
immediately because a "wide door for effective work" (1 Cor. 16:9) has opened
for him in Ephesus. To take advantage of the opening of this wide door (or
"great door," as rendered in some translations) is so appealing to Paul that he
decides to remain in Ephesus, at least for a while.[1]

These verses include a metaphor often used to describe one of the ways
God calls—the metaphor of an open door. It is not uncommon to hear people
describe God's call using this image, referring to God's "opening doors" or
"closing doors" when speaking of opportunities for ministry. Even Jesus used
the image to teach about the entrance to the kingdom of God:

> Then Jesus again said to them, "Truly, truly, I say to you, I am the
> door of the sheep. All who come before me are thieves and robbers,
> but the sheep did not listen to them. I am the door. If anyone enters
> by me, he will be saved and will go in and out and find pasture." (John
> 10:7-9, ESV)

And you may sometimes have heard it said that God used a "back door," or unexpected route, to open the way to some ministry.

God surely opens doors and closes doors to ministry service. And yes, God may use a "back door" of some type to achieve a mission or purpose he desires. In the passage opening this chapter, Paul feels led to pursue the "wide door" which has opened for him to preach and teach the gospel of Christ in Ephesus. Ephesus, a major city at that time, no doubt needed to hear this gospel message, and Paul is clearly thankful that such a wide door for his ministry has opened for him there.

Have you had opportunities for ministry where you felt that doors were clearly open or clearly closed? Have you ever seen good ministry accomplished, not in expected ways, but through a "back door" or alternate way?

Following are some suggestions relative to using the image of doors as a way to think about God's call. These examples are not exhaustive; instead, they illustrate ways to discern God's call from the avenues that are open to you.

1. *Doors, or paths for ministry, that are perceived as "wide open" can indicate a clear direction for ministry.*

There are times when God's direction for ministry is absolutely clear. We can be thankful for such times. When the path we should take is clear, it surely saves time and stress. One's sense of certainty may be the result of prayer, affirmations from others, or timely opportunities. Moreover, when our convictions are confirmed before we have even had the chance to pray about them, we feel convinced that our intended path of action is the correct one. When we are convinced that not only has a door opened for ministry, but a "wide door" at that, we can be more confident that we are on the right path. Not only did a door open for Paul to preach in Ephesus, but it presented an opportunity that he did not want to miss. It sometimes happens that wide doors for ministry just open before us.

2. *A door others think you should go through may not be the one God intends for you.*

Our text from 1 Corinthians suggests that Paul longed to return to Corinth as soon as possible and that the doors for ministry remained open for him there. He even speaks of plans to spend the winter in Corinth. The believers there are apparently dependable supporters of his ministry. But Paul believes that God has other immediate plans for him in Ephesus and that he would be making a mistake not to take advantage of this opportunity. Thus, Paul concludes that returning to Corinth will have to wait for a while.

Sometimes a door to a ministry that beckons you does not lead to where you are most needed at the time. Timing is an important component of a call. Sometimes the right opportunity comes at the right time. At other times the opportunity may be good, but for you the timing is not good. For example, a minister who receives an official ecclesiastical call to become the next minister of a church may conclude that accepting this call would result in hardships for his or her family, hardships that would not be fair to them. The Corinthians hoped initially that Paul would be coming to them soon, but Paul felt called to go to Ephesus first. Have you experienced good opportunities matching up with perfect timing? And have you also experienced opportunities arising when the timing was not the best? When good opportunities come at bad times, deciding what to do is more complicated. The wise course of action is to seek the counsel of trusted mentors and prayer partners while also spending time in prayer yourself.

3.   *You should be alert to factors that might pull you away from the doors God opens for you.*[2]

In the concluding phrase of the passage we've been discussing, Paul states that although a wide door has opened in Ephesus, "there are many adversaries" (1 Cor. 16:9). Even when wide doors open, obstacles and challenges do not automatically disappear. Clearly, Paul did not want these adversaries to block his new ministry, so he mentioned the need for Corinthian believers to pray for his new work. Even though he could not return to Corinth right away, he still needed the support of the faithful believers in Corinth.

The lesson here is an important one. You should take great care not to let things pull you away from the doors God opens, especially if you are convinced you should follow this leading. Pursuing formal theological education may serve as a good example. Should God open the door for you to begin a lifelong dream to enter seminary or divinity school, it is likely that many obstacles will come to mind as to why this undertaking seems impossible. Some reasons might be your age, family responsibilities, lack of resources, work schedules, or fears of becoming a student again.

However, nontraditional-age people who enter educational programs often find ways to make schedules and finances work. Unforeseen scholarship assistance, surprising church support, the blessing of learning new things, and the joy of new friendships all are huge rewards in such a venture. If at all possible, do not give up on the call you have experienced. If you persevere, you may find doors opening before you. Sometimes, indeed, "where there is a will, there is a way." This is especially true if it is God's will.

Additional Ways God Calls

The image of doors opening and closing provides a good introduction to looking at other ways God calls. Of course, there is no way to chronicle all the ways God can call persons to his service. Nevertheless, God uses a number of ways to summon servants to his work in ministry. Knowing some of them can be instructive.

1. *Live close to God and cultivate a receptive, listening spirit.*

I was once advised to "slow down to succeed," and I have often observed the benefit of this advice. The logic behind this counsel is that it is better to do a few things well than to accomplish many things in a mediocre manner. When serving as a pastor, I used to tell members of the church staff that I preferred they do one or two things well than to attempt many things with only mediocre results. And I have tried to pass this counsel on to my students.

This same logic applies to hearing and discerning a call from God. To discern God's movements in our lives, we often have to change places—not geographical places but emotional and spiritual places. The challenge is to alter an aggressive style of constant, busy activities to make time for being receptive, quiet, and discerning. Becoming in touch with the spiritual movements in our lives requires that we designate times each day to slow down, listen to God and discern his guidance for us. Thomas Merton said it this way: "Waste time with God."[3] Remember: Prayer is listening as well as speaking.

Finding the needed time for thoughtful meditation is hard but essential. This was one of the admirable qualities of Jesus. Although crowds surrounded him constantly, he would find time to withdraw to places where he could commune with God. He stepped away from crowds, ministry, and noise to find places for quiet, prayer, and discernment. Such times for listening, prayer, and meditation are essential in nurturing a relationship with God and understanding a call experience. God may use the Holy Spirit to reveal much to one who continually comes before him in such a manner. Is there a need in your life to become more disciplined at "changing places" for a while each day?

Two additional reflective activities may be helpful during times of prayer and meditation. First, one might reflect further on Frederick Buechner's challenge (mentioned earlier) to answer two questions about call. Buechner asked: "What do you love doing the most and what do you feel the world needs the most?"[4] Do your answers to these questions help you in defining your call?

Next, reflect on the spiritual gifts God has given you. The lists of spiritual gifts are given in three texts in the New Testament (Rom. 12:6-8; 1 Cor. 12:4-11; and 1 Cor. 12:28). Careful readers will notice that these lists are not identical. Select the list described in Romans 12:6-8, for example, and think deeply about how these gifts of the Holy Spirit apply to you and inform your calling. This will be time well spent.

Take steps now that will help you live closer to God by cultivating meditation times and a receptive spirit for God to reveal direction for your life. Reflect on the ways God has shaped you in the past and the spiritual gifts you have been given for the present. Clarification or confirmation of a call experience may result from these sacred meditations.

2. *God often calls in clear, unmistakable ways.*

Sometimes God's call comes in obvious, dramatic, and unmistakable ways. Such dramatic calls are seen, for example, in the calls of Moses and Saul of Tarsus. God spoke to Moses by means of the theophany of the burning bush and to Saul through his encounter with the resurrected Christ on the Damascus Road. Such dramatic calls can be experienced today even though most call experiences are more gradual and evolve over time. Thus, one should not feel shortchanged if a call experience is not as dramatic as that of Moses or Saul. But make no mistake about it: God can call persons in unmistakable, dramatic ways.

3. *Another way God calls is through the inspiration of texts in the Scriptures.*

Some people, in describing their call stories, share how God spoke directly to them through a text in Scripture. Ben Campbell Johnson writes that "the presence of God can come through a text in scripture in the same way that light fills a room."[5] John Killinger reminds all ministers to read the Bible "as if you are listening to it and not as if you wrote it."[6]

This is precisely what some persons report about their call experience. A passage of Scripture makes an unexpected and life-changing impact upon them. This impact is often so strong that it results in the clarification or confirmation of a call.

Of particular help, I believe, are the call stories of the Bible as illustrated in the previous chapter. There are many rich connections to make between these biblical stories and our stories. This, however, is not to minimize the impact of other texts in the Bible. As one seeks to live closer to God and to develop a receptive attitude in prayer and meditation, the next good step is to immerse oneself in the reading of Scriptures. Good things may happen. God continues to speak through the Bible to call persons into ministry. John Killinger offers another word of advice: "Read, read, read as though your intellectual and spiritual life depended on it."[7]

4. *God often calls persons to ministry or to service by simply revealing a need.*

In the call story of the prophet Isaiah (Isa. 6:1-8), God calls in this way. Isaiah, burdened by the news of the death of King Uzziah and the overwhelming threats of external aggressors against Israel, goes to the temple to worship. As Isaiah goes to worship out of his own need, God reveals the needs of others to him. Israel is in need of spiritual leadership, and so God asks, "Whom shall I send? Who will go for us?" (Isa. 6:1-8). Isaiah volunteers for this mission: "Here am I. Send me" (Isa. 6:8).

God's call often works in this way. He reveals a need and expects our faith, sensibilities, and judgments to take over. Churches see needs and respond. Chaplains see hurt and pain in suffering people and respond. So many good ministries take place because someone saw a need and responded.

God may place a need of the world or of people on your heart. The impact may be that you cannot help but help. This can be particularly true where the pain of others is involved. God can lead people to respond to the suffering and pain they see in those who are hurting. God still calls people to ministry through revealing the needs of others. Has God placed a need on your heart that you cannot escape?

5.   *God can call persons to ministry or service through the influence of others.*

Here is a wonderful way you may gradually discover a call to ministry. It can happen in various ways. You may have been invited to be a participant in a ministry already in progress and developed a great love for the work being done. The result may be that something blossoms in you and you feel called to this ministry full time. Or you may be inspired as the result of what others have noticed in you and in the spiritual gifts they have observed as you have been involved in a ministry. The influence of others can help you see in yourself what others see in you. These are all examples of how different people have discovered a call from God.

6.   *God's call can gradually grow clearer over time.*

While some calls from God are unmistakable, once-in-a-lifetime events, like those of Moses and Saul of Tarsus, most calls to Christian service are gradually discerned over time. If your call from God has been one of progressive revelation over the years, do not feel shortchanged. Divine calls discerned gradually are to be held in the same high regard as calls revealed in more dramatic fashion.

It should not be assumed that persons who experience their calls gradually do not have special revelations from God. Quite the opposite is true. Sacred and holy moments may have been numerous and powerful to these persons through the years. Like any called person, those whose call has come gradually may recall times when God's presence was powerful and moving. God's call may be just as clear in the lives of those who have had a Christian heritage and an active life of faith as it is to someone whose call is more dramatic. In fact, a faith-filled heritage should be celebrated and appreciated.

Sometimes, when testimonies about God's call are shared, those whose calls have been gradual often feel their experiences are uneventful compared to those whose testimonies describe more dramatic calls, such as repentance from grievous sins, serious addictions, or other destructive lifestyles. Give thanks to God if such things have not happened to you. You do not have to be "bad enough" to be called by God.

These, then, are some common ways God calls persons into ministry or service. They are not exhaustive; God's call can happen in many ways. In fact, call experiences may involve components of many of the ways listed above. Call experiences are clarifying events that can occur at various times and in various stages of life. The influences of others, experiences in ministry, and the guidance of mentors are all avenues whereby God's call can be discerned.

It is also helpful to be reminded that God's call can lead through winding paths. Traveling the path to the recognition of a call can take time. Unexpected detours and destinations can be part of the call experience. These can provide insightful lessons about God, about the spiritual needs of others, and about oneself. These insights are to be valued and can increase your love for God, for the mission of the church, and for other people. God can do great work through those who possess these traits and who believe that a "wide door for effective work" may open for them, as it did for Paul.

Adjustments to the Call

At the time of a call, a person does not have all he or she will need to fulfill it. Time is needed for a call experience to be fully processed. In Paul's case, he went to Arabia for a while after his dramatic call on the Damascus Road (Gal. 1:7). Even though his call was unmistakable, there were still things to learn and adjustments to be made. Paul needed time to reflect on all that had happened to him, to learn from other apostles, and to discover the mission God had selected him for. Learning from the other apostles was part of Paul's preparation. But he emphasized that he did not learn "his gospel" from the Jerusalem apostles but from Christ alone (Gal. 1:11-2:10). Paul wanted to make clear that his understanding of the gospel did not come from human mentors. But while he held fast to this position, he still needed to learn to value his associates in his ministry. And he ultimately did. Another example of Paul needing additional tutoring can be seen in his preparation for his missionary journeys, which did not begin until years later.

Paul had other adjustments to make as well, including his understanding of the risen Christ and the resurrection. He was converted during a time when he had been persecuting the Lord's people. What a change! He was to become an important leader of the people he had previously sought to persecute.

Such a change in perspective and awareness of others did not happen overnight.

Other adjustments Paul had to make were theological in nature. His belief that righteousness is gained through the keeping of the law, for example, would be challenged by the new teachings of Christ that salvation comes by faith and not by the law. Once Paul understood the essence of "salvation by faith as opposed to the law," he never tired of preaching it. But it surely took time for him to work this out in his mind. Another big turnaround for Paul was accepting that persons are all "one in Christ Jesus" (Gal. 3:28). Paul's skills in ministry to others, like his theological convictions, developed over time. And how blessed Christianity has been that they did.

The same is true today for those responding to a call from God. No one has all they need for effective ministry at the moment of responding positively to God's call. Examples of needed preparation might include biblical and theological study, along with developing specific ministry skills. We all have much to learn.

Questions for Discernment

1. Do you believe that God has opened doors or closed doors for you as you contemplated ministry? Can you describe how?

2. Of the various ways that God calls people described in this chapter, which one best fits your experience?

3. In responding to God's call, have you had to make adjustments? Have some of these adjustments affected your life plans and possibly your family's? Have some been adjustments in your theological understanding as you have studied God's word and sought to learn from others?

Notes

[1]The New International Version and the New King James Version of the Bible are two examples of translations that render this part of the verse as a "great door."

[2]I am indebted for insight into this passage from a sermon I heard via video preached by Dr. Joel Gregory at the Annual Meeting of the Baptist World Alliance in the summer of 2016.

[3]Johnson, *Hearing God's Call*, 15.

[4]Buechner, *Wishful Thinking*, 64.

[5]Johnson, *Hearing God's Call*, 37-38.

[6]John Killinger, *The Ministry Life: 101 Tips for New Ministers* (Macon, GA: Smyth & Helwys, 2013), 41-42.

[7]Ibid., 19-20.

CHAPTER FOUR

The Places God Calls: One Never Knows

Paul, an apostle—sent not from men nor by man,
but by Jesus Christ and God the Father
…To the churches in Galatia;
…To the saints in Ephesus;
…To all the saints in Christ Jesus at Philippi.
(Gal. 1:2; Eph. 1:1; Phil. 1:1)

Ordained ministers and laypersons who dedicate their lives to ministry often discover a delightful surprise along the journey: a sense of amazement and gratitude to God for the unexpected blessings experienced as a result of hearing and obeying God's call. Blessings they mention include the wonderful people they meet, the spiritual rewards, and the work they accomplish during their experiences in ministry. Such testimonies reinforce a theme of this book: namely, that it is worth a life to be a minister. And one does not have to have accumulated long years of service to discover these blessings. This benefit can be recognized early and often in a minister's life.

This certainly has been my experience in vocational ministry. My years as an ordained minister have been more rewarding than I ever imagined possible. In my career, I have been privileged to serve two churches as pastor and more than twenty churches as interim pastor. My experiences as an interim pastor have been a part of my vocation as a professor. And I never imagined that I would serve for fifteen years as the founding dean of a divinity school. How grateful I am for all these opportunities for service.

Unfortunately, not all who feel called have a similar experience. Vocational ministry does not work out for some, even though they are called and often have the needed educational credentials. Such disappointments are painful and should be a reminder to those of us employed in ministry to open doors of service, when possible, to those who seek opportunities to serve but cannot find them. Thankfully, most who prepare for a vocational ministry do find opportunities to serve.

Do you recall our earlier discussion of the calls of Abraham and Sarah to be the first of a new covenant people (Gen. 11:30-23:20)? As Abraham and Sarah dealt with their inability to have children, God's call came to them—and what a call it was. They were "to become forebearers of a new covenant people, to go to a land that God would show them, and to have descendants more numerous than the stars (Gen. 12:1-3: 15:5-6)." By the conclusion of their story later in Genesis (and years later in their lives), the astonishing prophecy they received unfolded in ways they could never have imagined. The childless couple became parents, and they became the spiritual ancestors of Judaism, Christianity, and Islam. Could they have ever imagined such a legacy, with all the difficulties they encountered? When one is obedient to God's call, one never knows all God may have planned. The legacy of the faithfulness of Abraham and Sarah is remembered in several books of the New Testament. For example, Paul pays tribute to them in his Epistle to the Romans, expressing his admiration for Abraham's faithfulness:

> What then are we to say was gained by Abraham, our ancestor according to the flesh?...Abrahambelieved God and it was reckoned to him as righteousness. ...No distrust made him waver concerning the promise of God, but he grew stronger in his faith as he gave glory to God, being fully convinced that God was able to do what he had promised. (4:1, 3, 20-21)

With God's help, other characters in the Bible achieve goals that surprise them—and others.

- Upon reading the account of Moses being called at the burning bush (Exod. 3:11-4:17) and hearing Moses giving excuses as to why he should not lead the mission to free the Hebrew slaves, who could have ever predicted the dramatic exodus from Egypt that he would eventually lead?
- Upon hearing the young Gideon tell God that his clan was the weakest in the tribe of Manasseh and that he was the least in his family (Judg. 6:15), who could imagine that Gideon would lead Israel to great victories and bring peace to the land for nearly forty years? (Judg. 8:28)

- Upon hearing Simon Peter deny his personal acquaintance with Jesus three times in Jerusalem in the days before the crucifixion (Matt. 26: 69-75), who could have ever predicted his strong preaching of the resurrected Christ at Pentecost only a few weeks later? (Acts 2:14-39)
- Upon hearing the murderous threats of Saul of Tarsus against Christian believers in the early chapters of Acts (Acts 9:1-4), who could have predicted that this zealot would become the great apostle Paul, who would lead the Christian mission to the Gentiles and author many of the books in the New Testament?

You never know all that God has in store for those who are obedient to his call. And the surprising power of the Almighty to change the lives of characters in the Bible continues to be evident in the lives of called persons today. Read now three call stories of persons whose lives were changed in ways they never imagined at the outset of their ministries. As you read these accounts, be alert to lessons from their stories that may help you "read" your story with different eyes.

Alta's Story: Progressive Revelation

As a young girl, Alta sensed God's call in her life. Later, as a young woman, Alta felt a more specific call. She came to believe that God was calling her to help families, especially young couples as they prepared for marriage and a future life together. Having earned a baccalaureate degree, Alta also earned a master's degree in counseling to prepare to work with families.

But Alta's desired ministry path and vocational choice did not happen right away. A financially viable job that would have allowed her to begin this ministry did not materialize as quickly as she would have liked. Instead, she took a position in business, one which developed into a successful career. Steeped in the corporate climate of pursuing success, she remained there for several years. But despite her successes, Alta never forgot her original calling and ministry goals.

Alta eventually left the corporate world to become president of a family-owned construction company, where her family now needed her business and leadership skills. She remained in this work for some time. But eventually the urgings of her original desires to enter the ministry convinced her to consider the call God had given her years before.

Soon after retiring from the business world, Alta enrolled in a divinity school near her home and discovered that the more steps she took to fulfill God's call, the more powerful the call became. She would later describe her time in divinity school as one of the greatest life-changing events she had ever experienced.

Upon graduation from divinity school, Alta determined to be intentional over the next months in listening for God's direction for her life. In August of the summer following graduation, she received an invitation from a local church to become an interim minister to college students. She accepted this opportunity. Soon, this position was made full-time, and it was not long until Alta was promoted to associate pastor of the congregation. She was now perfectly situated to minister to families in her church and community.

Alta calls her journey "progressive revelation." God did not position her in the ministry context she desired at first, but, ultimately, she did arrive at this place of ministry where she served joyfully for many years. She is now convinced that God honored her calling in his time.

From corporate executive to company president to divinity student to ordained minister, Alta never gave up on her calling, and, in God's timing, it came to fulfillment. You never know what God has planned for one obedient to his call.

Jackson's Story: A Search for Truth and Mission

As a boy growing up in Ghana, Jackson knew that serving God in some way would be a part of his adult life. Although he felt no leading as a young man to enter full-time vocational ministry, he tried to serve God as a faithful disciple. Jackson was gifted in science, math, and writing. Because of these gifts, he decided to pursue a degree in engineering, which he completed. He then started an advanced degree online but abandoned this pursuit after a short time. Jackson was starting to discern that God was calling him to a different work.

Jackson's call was experienced as feeling a burden for others placed on his heart. He became increasingly concerned for the spiritual welfare of his homeland and worried that a form of the gospel message called "the prosperity gospel" was becoming widely accepted by the people of Ghana. He wanted them to hear a truer version of the gospel of Christ and his teachings. Some relief came to Jackson's spirit when he read a book by Billy Graham titled *Peace With God*. Graham's book led Jackson to become more intentional about seeking God's will for his future.

Over time, a vision of a needed ministry in Ghana developed in Jackson's mind and heart. He felt the call to prepare himself to found a seminary to educate and train pastors to serve churches in his native country.

Jackson's call was heartfelt and his vision noble, but it would require great sacrifice. To gain the knowledge and theological credentials he knew he would need would require looking abroad for study. The hurdles appeared daunting—the selection of a theological school to attend, the expense and red tape of travel to the United States, the costs of tuition and living expenses, immigration issues, and separation from his family and fiancée.

Jackson was not deterred. He was committed to his calling and to the vision God had given him. He came to the United States to begin his theological studies with only one travel bag and a laptop. Even his departure from Ghana was characterized by uncertainty and drama involving proper visa documentation and other red tape that might have caused less determined individuals to give up. But Jackson's profound faith and genuine piety sustained him.

Several years have now passed. Jackson is nearing completion of his theological degree and plans to pursue further graduate study. When he returns to Ghana, these degrees will qualify him to establish an accredited and reputable seminary program in his home country.

God has yet to write the ending to Jackson's story. The journey has been hard at times. Jackson reports that he was down "to some bread and half a coke" at times. But even during those times, he drew strength from the words of Jesus in the New Testament:

> Meanwhile his disciples urged him, "Rabbi, eat something." But he (Jesus) said to them: "I have food to eat that you know nothing about. My food is to do the will of him who sent me and to finish his work." (John 4:31-34)

Although his journey is unfinished, Jackson is amazed at the supportive networks he has found in the United States. The people who have helped him, the knowledge he has gained, and the friendships he has made have been blessings that he never imagined he would find. Church families in America now support him and want to continue to help him upon his return to Ghana. Jackson's experience illustrates that you never know what God has in store when you are obedient to his call.

Lynn's Story: From Police Officer to Ordained Minister

Lynn is a winsome young woman who has changed career paths as a result of God's call on her life. Her story also makes clear that God's call can come to those who did not grow up in the church.

As Lynn progressed through college, she felt she had settled on a career path for her life—law enforcement. She completed her degree at North Carolina State University in Raleigh, North Carolina. She then entered the police academy and graduated as a certified police officer. Her first position was with the public safety unit of her alma mater. Lynn believed that she was on her way in her chosen career. But God had other plans.

A move to another state and some unfortunate life events led Lynn to a "season in the wilderness," a time she gave to reflection, study, and prayer. This season of reflection convinced her to return to her home in Fayetteville, North Carolina, where she came under the influence of a spiritual mentor, the Reverend Jesse Timmons. This able Christian pastor became to Lynn what Eli was to Samuel.

Over time, Lynn renewed her dedication to God, trusting in his love and grace to reveal a new life direction for her. As her openness to God's will increased, so did the convictions she had about a possible career in ministry. It was not long until the conviction of God's call to ministry blossomed in her life.

Lynn subsequently answered a call to ministry and enrolled in a nearby divinity school. According to her, she "knew she had to be there but did not know all the reasons why." She was successful in her studies, graduated, and eventually presented herself for ordination to the gospel ministry. A former police officer was now officially an ordained minister.

One vision Lynn kept in her heart was a conviction that she would one day serve on the staff of the divinity school that nurtured her. This vision became a reality, as she now serves as a teacher, staff member, and minister to students in the school. In addition, she has a full schedule of preaching, serving churches, and providing leadership to congregations and other organizations. She has a rewarding and meaningful life as an ordained minister.

Lynn is amazed at the change of career paths she experienced. She can hardly believe the places she has been invited to preach, the invitations for leadership she has received, and that she has earned a Doctor of Ministry degree and had the joy and satisfaction of writing a book. At one time in her life, she could have never imagined such a career. Now, her advice to others is to "bloom where you are planted."

Important Lessons from Call Stories

New chapters in life and ministry like those described above happen all the time for those who hear and respond to God's call. Living out God's call can happen in many ways, as the stories of Alta, Jackson, and Lynn illustrate.

But an element common in these three accounts is that all three individuals were responding to the needs of others. Remember: When God calls us, he calls us to help others. Alta's desire was to minister to hurting families. Jackson's hope was to bring wholesome interpretations of the gospel message to the people of his homeland. Lynn's desire was to minister to ministerial students just as she had been ministered to.

Note that God's call is rarely a text message. Most call stories feature winding paths, gradual breakthroughs in discernment, and helpful mentors along the way. No two call stories are exactly alike. Paths to discernment take time. God calls and leads in many ways. While you never know all God has in store, you can know of his presence all along the journey.

How Can I Know?

Perhaps the number one question asked by persons who think they may be called is, "How can I know this call is from God?" If this question has surfaced in your mind, don't be troubled. Seeking confirmation of a call can be a sign of honesty and humility. Your wish to be certain that the call has divine origins is admirable. You may also be anxious that your call may have some other source or motivation.

It is natural to seek assurance that the decisions we make are justified. Such feelings are present, for example, when choosing a university or graduate school, when considering a new job, or when purchasing a new home. We try to ensure that the decisions we make are the correct ones. The same dynamic is at work when considering a call from God. We want to be sure that the call is from God and that we are responding correctly.

The good news is that there are ways to know that a call is from God. While there is no single way of confirmation, God has provided reliable and trustworthy means to give us confidence in his call. Responding to a call from God not only involves the best reasoning of mind and intellect but also the inspirational elements of faith and obedience. All these components working together can yield excitement, spiritual vitality, and personal energy. Answering a call from God is an ongoing process, not a static one, and it can be full of personal blessings.

Before discussing the ways of knowing if a call is from God, it may be helpful to remember that many of the prophets and disciples in the Bible sought the same confirmations you may be seeking. Let us consider one person from each category: the prophet Moses and the disciple Thomas.

Moses, the great leader of Israel, experienced a dramatic calling from God on Mt. Sinai in the episode of the burning bush. The full text of Moses' call experience (Exod. 3:1–4:17) reveals that he was full of questions about his call from God to return to Egypt to lead the Israelites out of bondage. Moses was not sure he was the best person to lead this mission. At one point in his dramatic call experience, he inquired of God: "If I come to the Israelites and say to them, *'The God of your ancestors has sent me to you,' and they ask me, 'What is his name?' What shall I say to them?"* (Exod. 3:13).

And later, in the same revelation, he sought more assurance: *"But suppose they do not believe me or listen to me, but say, the LORD did not appear to you." The LORD said to him, "What is that in your hand?" Moses replied, "A staff"* (Exod. 4:1-2).

Moses was seeking to interpret and process this overwhelming call from God. He wanted certainty that, should he accept this mission, divine presence and assurances would be with him. Going back to Egypt was risky for Moses because of his history with Pharaoh. God answered his concerns, assuring Moses of his presence and power at every stage of the upcoming challenges. Moses obeyed this call, and we know what, with God's help, he achieved.

And who can forget perhaps the best biblical example of a disciple of Jesus searching for certainty—the experience of Thomas after the resurrection. That a person could rise from the dead following a brutal execution seemed beyond the realm of possibility to Thomas: So the other disciples told him, *"We have seen the Lord." But he said to them, "Unless I see the mark of the nails in his hands, and put my finger in the mark of the nails and my hand in his side, I will not believe"* (John 20:25).

Thomas wanted certainty that this news of a resurrected Jesus was true. He wanted to see Jesus in person and determine for himself if the reports were accurate. And this face-to-face meeting with Jesus happened a week after his demand when the risen Lord appeared to Thomas (John 20:26-29). What a dramatic encounter this was. Jesus did not chastise Thomas for his questioning. Instead, he reached out and challenged him to greater faith in the future.

We know that we live in a different age and culture than did Moses and Thomas. Nevertheless, when we encounter God's calls today, we may yearn for authentication and assurance, as did Moses and Thomas. The good news is that God provides some ways of knowing. As you process your calling, remember two important facts. First, God does not desire certainty as our primary response to him. What God wants from us is faith. Strive always to keep faith in and obedience to God ahead of any desire for certainty. Second, remember that believers are never without the certainty of God's love and of his wanting the best for his children.

Let us now examine some of the ways authentic calls from God can be confirmed.

Knowing Through Revelation

One of the ways God confirms callings, as well as one of the ways he calls, is through revelations. Revelations from God can be dramatic and unmistakable, such as Moses seeing a "bush burning but not consumed" (Exod. 3:2-3) or Saul of Tarsus experiencing a "blinding light and the voice of the risen Lord"

(Acts 9:3-6). Other revelations can be more natural, like holy moments or times of deeply felt spiritual experiences. Intellectual breakthroughs can sometimes be revelations from God. An example would be when one receives greater insight and clarity into God's ways and works through serious thought and reflection.

Sacred revelations occur when the presence of God is experienced in an extraordinary manner. There is usually a "powerful sense of the holy" within or about a person, as well as a sense of God's presence. Such moments are holy. Many persons of faith have had these kinds of experiences with God. Confirmations of a call may occur in such moments.

Revelations from God can occur in different settings. Some may be experienced in a worship service, on a retreat, in times of private prayer, or even in a crisis situation, such as a hospitalization after a traumatic accident or illness. God can reveal truths to persons in many ways, and confirmation of a call may happen at these times.

Simon Peter's confession of Christ as Messiah at Caesarea Philippi provides a clear example of knowing as a result of revelation:

> Now when Jesus came into the district of Caesarea Philippi, he asked his disciples, "Who do people say the Son of Man is?" And they said, "Some say John the Baptist, but others Elijah, and still others Jeremiah or one of the prophets." He said to them, "But who do you say that I am?" Simon Peter answered, "You are the Messiah, the Son of the living God." And Jesus answered him, "Blessed are you, Simon son of Jonah! For flesh and blood have not revealed this to you, but my Father in heaven." (Matt. 16:13-17)

Jesus indicates to Peter that his recognizing of Christ as the Messiah has not come through human sources (flesh and blood) but through a revelation from God the Father. God can reveal knowledge and confirm callings through revelation.

My call experience falls in this category. As a sophomore in college, I was unhappy and unfulfilled in my chosen major. I began a search for more clear direction for my life. Months later, a holy encounter with God, a revelation, came to me as I sat in a worship service in required chapel. I did not hear any loud voice from God, but I did experience an overwhelming sense of the holy.

I discerned God speaking to my heart that the decision I was considering—to devote my life to Christian ministry—was his will for me. These exhilarating moments provided the answer for which I had been searching. It was a spirit-filled encounter with God. This confirmation experience was not the only one I have had, but it was a powerful one at a time when I needed it. God confirms his call in similar ways for his servants during the course of their service. Today, years later, I still recall this holy encounter in a college chapel service as one of the decisive moments in my life. There was no dramatic "thunder and lightning," only holy minutes connecting with God. It was knowing through revelation.

Have you had moments or experiences of revelations from God? Have any of these "holy encounters or moments" brought confirmation of your call?

Knowing Through Reason

In addition to knowing by means of revelation or holy encounters with God, confirmations of call may also come through human reasoning. Reason and revelation should go hand in hand in a believer's life. To affirm the presence and power of holy revelation from God is not to undermine the gifts of reason and discernment. Reason and revelation are both gifts from God and should work in concert. A thinking and learning disciple needs both. To understand the ways of God, the nature of his character, the ways he works, and the needs of the world calls for clear thinking. Knowledge of God and confirmation of his call can come through reason and discernment as well as through holy revelations. Revelation and reason are not opposites; they are companions. Sometimes, to confirm a call, good reasoning is all you need. I think God equips us to figure some things out on our own.

Knowing By Doing

Assurances of a divine call can also be confirmed through action. Stated another way, knowing can come from doing.

Ben Campbell Johnson observes that knowing by doing is a reversal of the way we normally think. The traditional pattern is to know first, then base our actions on that knowledge. Johnson suggests that, relative to confirmation of divine calls, it often happens in the opposite way: We act or obey in order to know.[1] He cites a biblical example:

In the church at Antioch, the small group of disciples had no way of knowing the outcome of their obedience. They prayed over Barnabas and Saul and sent them forth on their mission. First they obeyed, and then they knew.[2]

Campbell's point is that discernment is not collecting a lot of information about God. Rather, it sometimes results from doing the will of God. Action leads to knowing. This is a strong way of knowing a call is from God.

Becoming involved in ministry activities can bring confirmations of your calling. Serving in an internship while in college or graduate school, accepting a part-time position in a church, participating in mission trips, volunteering in hospitals, or working for social justice causes can all be ways to confirm a calling. What a great principle to embrace—knowing by doing. Don't be afraid to take action based on your best thinking and the open doors before you. Get busy serving God and helping people, and then listen for what the Holy Spirit may be teaching you through this service.

Knowing Through Prayer, Study, and Reflection

Of course, prayer is an essential element in confirmation of a call. Doug Koskela recommends letting our prayers be marked by attentiveness, honesty, and discipline.[3] **Attentiveness** in prayer means to come with an open mind fully focused on communing with God. **Honesty** in prayer means being your true self when you pray; it means cultivating skills in asking and listening. **Discipline** in prayer means committing to daily prayer, Scripture reading, and reflection, even when you may not feel like it. Honest, attentive, disciplined prayer, says Koskela, puts an individual in a good position to discern God's will.[4]

Study and reflection are also indispensable. During times of meditation, it is amazing how one's vision is clarified and insights unfold about what one should be doing in ministry. As your meditation times increase, potential paths for ministry often start becoming clearer.

Knowing Through Communal Discernment, Wise Mentors, and the Influence of Others

A helpful step in confirming a call is through counsel from wise mentors and the guidance of other trusted friends. God can work through others to give persons the confirmation they need.

The teachings of your church tradition regarding call might be helpful to you as you seek to understand God's call. Your church family may also appreciate the opportunity to hear you talk about your call journey while encouraging you to follow your call and supporting you in ministry.

Seeking the counsel of wise mentors is also invaluable in clarifying a call experience. Such mentors may be pastors, professors, or others you consider to be wise and discerning. Some of these individuals may be living the life you are considering. They may have experienced a journey similar to yours and can share wisdom collected over the years. Conferring with others about your calling should not be overlooked.

The steps discussed above can be reliable ways to confirm a divine calling. They are not exhaustive, but they indicate ways God has worked in other calling experiences. Seek direction from God but not complete and final answers. Follow the best light you have at the time. Allow room for trusting God and living by faith. You may be surprised at the doors God opens for you.

Questions for Discernment

1. What is your call story like? Does it feature any winding paths? What has been your experience with revelations from God? What lessons have you deduced from your story?

2. What do you think of the idea of "knowing by doing?"

3. In your Christian journey, do you have a "you never know" story?

4. Have you put your call story in writing? At times in ministry you will be asked to share your call story, either in writing or orally. Become proficient at both.

Notes

[1]Ben Campbell Johnson, *Hearing God's Call*, 104.
[2]Ibid., 103.
[3]Doug Koskela, *Calling and Clarity*, 75.
[4]Ibid., 78.

CHAPTER FIVE

Should I Pursue Ordination?

While they were worshiping the Lord and fasting, the Holy Spirit said,
"Set apart for me Barnabas and Saul for the work to which I have called them."
Then, after fasting and praying they laid their hands on them and sent them off.
(Acts 13:2-3)

It is a thrilling experience to acknowledge God's call and to respond with excitement and dedication. Equal joy comes in sharing this commitment with others and in imagining what a future life in ministry might be like.

Once God's call has been discerned, the question of whether to seek formal ordination by the church will probably arise. This question can surface at any time after a call is felt. It may come soon after the experience or much later, perhaps even after divinity school studies are completed. It may occur while one is still in school or when a first position in ministry is accepted. Whenever the question arises, the decision should not be rushed. The Scriptures teach the church "to not lay hands on anyone hastily" (1 Tim. 5:22). And not all calls from God to ministry require ordination.

Sources of guidance are available to those considering whether to pursue the path to ordination. Among these sources are one's own thinking and praying about the matter, published materials about the meaning of ordination, and the trusted counsel of wise mentors. All can be invaluable in helping one reach a decision about ordination.

Call and ordination are closely related but are separate matters. Not all ministries require ordination; one does not have to be ordained to have a meaningful or important ministry. On the other hand, some ministries of the church are ordained ministries. It is important to understand the close connections and clear differences between the two.

This chapter seeks to describe these distinctions and to offer suggestions about questions to consider in deciding whether or not to seek ordination.

What Is Ordination?

Formal ordination to the Christian ministry is a specific rite through which the church, in a special service, sets apart a ministerial candidate (sometimes called the ordinand) for service to God and the church as an ordained minister. An ordination service is a public recognition of one's private call to ministry.[1] The church conducting the ordination service is both setting apart the ministerial candidate for service and endorsing him or her for the church's ministry. The individual being ordained is dedicating himself or herself to the service of God and to the ministry of the church.

The word "ordain" means "to set apart."[2] Ordination does not admit one into a superior class of clergy. Quite the opposite is true. The ordinand is set apart for a church-related vocation or ministry, not to a status above or below others. Ordination is all about dedication to service for God. Generally, an ordained person is set apart for a specific ministry, such as preaching or missions. In recent years, some ordinations have been based on a more generic "call to ministry." More will be said about this later. Ordination is a call to servanthood, not to status or power. It is not a credential for ministry, as is a theological degree. Ideally, ordination seeks the person rather than the person seeking ordination.

Ordination services of worship tend to be celebratory. The ordained person is surrounded by fellow believers, family members, mentors, and friends. All are there to support, encourage, and affirm the ordinand.

These services include praises to God, vows, exhortations to faithful service, prayers for the ordinand, and the biblical ritual of the laying on of hands. The title of "Reverend" is conveyed upon ordination.

Ordination services for clergy are generally held for one ministerial candidate at a time. Ordination services for laity can include several persons, as in the Baptist ceremony for ordaining deacons. The themes of dedication to God, to the church, and to the needs of others characterize both types of service.

Ordination policies and practices vary among religious traditions and denominations. However, most denominations practice some form of ordination.[3] Baptists, for example, believe that ordination is a local church matter. This belief stems from the Baptist principle that each local church is autonomous. While Baptists may include associational or denominational representatives in examining candidates, it is the local church that ordains. Other church traditions or denominations specify ordination guidelines in accordance with their respective church polities. For example, Methodists, Presbyterians, and Anglicans have multi-step processes for ordination that may take years to complete.

For Baptists, the practice of ordination is usually less structured. After an ordination council is satisfied that a candidate's call is genuine and that the candidate's doctrine and educational preparation are sound, an ordination service is planned. Whether ordination councils are constituted from within a single church, from a denominational association or district, or from one of these groups but including members suggested by the candidate, the panel may request written responses to questions about the candidate's call and about his/her understanding of doctrine. The responses must be submitted in writing before the ordination review. Answering these questions in writing requires candidates to think seriously and honestly about the significant step they are taking. The written responses also provide the ordination council with helpful information about the candidate from which to formulate questions.

While it is not the purpose of this chapter to instruct those who plan the details of an ordination service, it may be helpful to future ordinands to be aware of a few matters that can be meaningful.

1. Great care should be taken to recognize the family of the ministerial candidate during the ordination service. This recognition may occur during the moments for welcome and introductions, at the times for prayers and blessings, or in a fellowship period following the worship experience. In addition, the spouse of the candidate, if there is one, is generally included during the part of the service called "the laying on of hands." This is done by having him or her sit or stand beside the candidate.

2. In an ordination service, candidates are often presented with symbols of their new office as an ordained minister. Such symbols might include a new Bible, a ministerial robe or stole, a framed Certificate of Ordination, or sacramental symbols such as a communion set or shepherd's staff. Ordinands are sometimes asked about their preference of an ordination gift.

A newer trend in some modern ordination services is the practice of some candidates to present themselves for ordination on the declaration of a call to ministry in general, as opposed to a call to a specific ministry, such as "a call to preach" or "a call to missions." Formerly, at least among Baptists, ordination was not allowed until one had been called to a specific pastoral role.

To present oneself for ordination on the statement of a call to ministry could be only a semantic issue or it could indicate the varieties of ministry opportunities available to prospective ministers today. In addition, this trend could also indicate that a person has a strong commitment to ministry but is uncertain about a specific vocational choice. In general, there is little cause for worry about this trend. Some excellent pastors, for example, never thought they would be pastors. The same can be said for other ministry professions.

Because ordination initiates one into a lifetime to service, both the candidate seeking ordination and the council and/or congregation ordaining the candidate should plan for the service with integrity and humility and execute it with reverence and celebration.

Biblical Backgrounds

Ordination in the Old Testament

The practice of ordination has Old Testament roots. The book of Exodus includes an account of God's instructions to Moses concerning the selecting and setting apart of priests. Priests were needed to provide spiritual leadership and maintain order among the Israelites, a tribe recently freed from bondage in Egypt and now living in the wilderness. Here is one passage describing how priests were to be ordained, anointed, and set apart by their vestments:

> For Aaron's sons you shall make tunics and sashes and headdresses; you shall make them for their glorious adornment. You shall put them on your brother Aaron, and on his sons with him, and shall anoint them and ordain them and consecrate them, so that they may serve me as priests. (Exod. 28:40-41)

These instructions from God to Moses suggest the Israelites' need for spiritual guidance. Echoes of this commissioning of Aaron—"to anoint, to ordain, and to consecrate"—can still be heard in some elements of ordination services today. John I. Durham, in his commentary on Exodus in the Word Biblical Commentary, points out that the Hebrew expression translated "to ordain" literally means "to fill the hand" (Exod. 28:41; 29:9, 33,35; Lev. 8:33), while the word for "consecrate" is from *qadash*, which means "to set apart" and "make holy."[4] It is clear that Aaron and his sons were "set apart" for their service as priests. This literal translation of "ordained" makes us aware of all the things a minister's hands may have to hold and juggle in representing God's claim on his people and in carrying the people's petitions to God.

Another well-known story from the Old Testament still applicable to ordinations today is that of Moses passing on the mantle of leadership to his successor, Joshua. Although this event might be considered more of a commissioning than an ordination, part of Joshua's role was to provide religious leadership for Israel. In this story, the ritual of "the laying on of hands" is carried out. This ritual persisted through the era of the New Testament and is still practiced today. The account of the laying on of hands to make Joshua's leadership official is reported in both Numbers 27:15-23 and Deuteronomy 34:9. Here is the account from Numbers 27:

> Moses spoke to the LORD, saying, "Let the LORD, the God of the spirits of all flesh, appoint someone over the congregation who shall go out before them, who shall lead them out and bring them in, so that the congregation of the LORD may not be like sheep without a shepherd." So the LORD said to Moses, "Take Joshua, son of Nun, a man in whom is the spirit, and lay your hands upon him; have him stand before Eleazer the priest and all the congregation, and commission him in their sight." (vv. 15-19)

This passage illustrates elements seen in modern ordination services. Among these are affirmations of God's call, the selection of a worthy candidate, the presence of God's spirit within the person, presentation of the candidate before a congregation, and the laying on of hands. In the previous passage about Aaron and his sons, is it a stretch for us to see a precedent for the wearing of appropriate vestments to signal the office of a priest or minister? In sum, ordination practices today still reflect some of the practices and rituals recorded in the selection of Old Testament priests and leaders.

In his book *Who Will Go For Us? An Invitation to Ordained Ministry*, Dennis Campbell offers a helpful explanation of the meaning of the laying on of hands:

The laying on of hands was an authorizing of leadership by one generation for another. The hands passed on responsibility and accountability. Those who had hands laid upon them were commissioned to lead in accordance with the tradition; and to lead into the future, with the guidance of God's spirit, whose presence was invoked with prayer. Those chosen were intended to be worthy of the trust of the people.[5]

Ceremonies like the ones described above do not appear to have been present in the calling and commissioning of the prophets of the Old Testament. Their commissioning moments seem to have been between them and God. Isaiah's call (Isa. 6:1-8) serves as an example. God calls, and Isaiah responds. Isaiah's ministry begins shortly thereafter. Even though no ceremony was carried out, the Old Testament prophets were clearly empowered for their ministries.

Ordination in the New Testament

The New Testament says little about the practice of ordination. The word "ordain" appears in some verses in particular translations of the New Testament, but the meaning in these verses is usually something other than the idea of setting one apart for ministry.[6] Moreover, the New Testament makes no mention of separating clergy and laity into different classes of people. This development evolved later in church history.[7]

What we do find in the New Testament is the thoughtful calling out of church leaders by the faith communities. Individuals judged to be qualified for leadership roles in the church were "set apart" and commissioned for their ministries. Examples include the appointment of elders (Titus 1:5), the anointing of priests (Heb. 5:1, 4), and the sending of new missionaries (Acts 14:2-3). The two letters to Timothy (1 and 2 Timothy) are longer but similar examples, describing Paul's thoughtful and extensive pastoral counsel to Timothy about how to lead his life and conduct his ministry work.

In the Book of Acts and in the Epistles to Timothy, we find that both the Hebrew followers of Christ and their Hellenistic converts adopt rituals similar to those found in the Old Testament to select and set apart spiritual leaders.

- Seeing a need for servants who would minister to the needs of widows and others, this early band of Christians set apart prototype deacons, identifying believers "of good repute, full of spirit and wisdom" and then setting them apart by "laying their hands upon them" (Acts 6:1-6).

- Also in the Book of Acts, we find that after a period of fasting and praying, Saul and Barnabas are set apart for their first missionary journey by the laying on of hands (13:1-3).
- In 1 Timothy 4:14, Paul reminded Timothy of his spiritual gifts and of the elders commissioning him through the laying on of hands.
- In 2 Timothy 1:6, Paul voiced a personal plea to Timothy to grow the gifts that God had given him and to remember that he had been blessed by a laying on of hands.

Thus, in the New Testament, some early practices used to consecrate leaders in the Old Testament are still being used: the setting apart of worthy candidates, the endorsement by a community of faith, and the laying on of hands. These components are visible even in the absence of a formal ordination service.

As the church grew in the years after the era of the New Testament, its organization gradually became more formal and structured, including specific services of the ordination of priests and ministers. But regardless of the level of formality, ordination candidates are to become trustworthy servants who can represent God to the people and the people to God.

Contemporary Questions Related to Ordination

Deciding to seek formal ordination to the ministry by a church is a big decision. Many questions can surface when you are trying to make this decision. Although it is not exhaustive, the following list of questions and responses may help you decide whether pursuing a path toward ordination is right for you.

1. *What are the qualifications for ordination?*

Although qualifications for ordination vary among denominations and even among congregations within a denomination, two are essential: a genuine conversion to faith in Christ (a salvation experience) and a call from God to enter the ministry (a calling testimony). These are usually the first two criteria explored in an ordination council. Ordination candidates should be prepared to share these two experiences with any ordaining council or committee.

Additional qualifications include excellent moral character, doctrinal soundness, educational preparation, and affirmation by the church conducting the ordination. More will be said about some of these qualifications later.

Another important qualification is being capable of handling the job. Ministers of the church need a strong work ethic and the physical and emotional capacity to handle the work. Dr. Daniel Aleshire, former Executive Director of the Association of Theological Schools, highlighted this aspect of a minister's vocation in a commissioning service at Campbell University Divinity School in 2003. He challenged students "to love God, love the people, and do the work."[8] The willingness and capacity to do the work are essential qualifications for ministry service.

2. *Is ordination really necessary? Why ordain anyone? Is it not true that all Christians are called to service?*

These are good questions. While it is true that all Christians are called to be servants of God, there are good reasons why the church needs ordained ministers.

First, churches need leaders well-versed in the Bible and in the history and doctrine of the church. In addition, the church needs leaders equipped to guide it in its work, growth, and service. Because of these varied demands, not just anyone can provide effective leadership. Effective ministers need skills in teaching, preaching, and counseling. Thus, not only does ordination serve as a rite of passage to affirm those whom God has called to this work, but preparing for ordination creates a pool of effective church leaders. Because most churches need more leaders than they have, churches should encourage the calling out and equipping of more lay leaders.

In addition, many tasks performed by church ministers are done most effectively by those with the proper educational preparation. The tasks of preaching and teaching, for example, are most effectively carried out by those who have studied the body of knowledge undergirding these ministries. A minister wants to be accurate and biblically correct in what he or she preaches and teaches. Good preaching, teaching, and leading require learning. Ordination affirms that a candidate has this type of preparation. Similar preparation should be expected of those who design and lead worship, administer the ordinances, and guide Christian education programs. Formal ordination recognizes both the call to ministry and the preparation of those answering the call.

Third, ordination is necessary for the various sacramental and legal dimensions of a minister's work. Most churches prefer that their ministers who preach regularly, perform baptisms, conduct weddings, and administer the ordinances be ordained clergy. In the case of performing wedding ceremonies, state law generally requires that the officiating minister be ordained in order for the marriage to be recognized as legal.

3. *Does every called person, clergy or laity, have to be ordained?*

No. Calling and ordination are separate matters. Not all called persons need to be ordained. One does not have to be ordained to have a needed and effective ministry. Examples of such ministries include social service ministries, church staff positions, university religion professors, chaplains, denominational workers, and leaders in para-church ministries. However, persons serving in such positions sometimes choose to be ordained. They want to be recognized as ordained ministers. Nevertheless, there are many ways to serve God and the church that do not require ordination.

4. *Are there educational requirements for ordination?*

In most instances, the answer is yes. Churches generally expect persons who fill ministry positions to be educationally qualified. This expectation has changed and continues to change. Not that long ago, it was common for persons to be ordained with little or no educational preparation. But now the majority of those hoping to be ordained are seeking educational credentials—in particular, degrees in theological education. Education brings richer content to one's ministry. The same holds true with respect to other ministerial duties, such as leadership, counseling, or music ministry. Educational preparation increases one's effectiveness and impact. Increasingly, ordination councils will be looking for and affirming candidates who are not only committed believers but are educationally prepared to serve as ministers.

5. *In many churches today, traditional routines and patterns of church life are changing. How are these trends, such as contemporary styles of worship and more informality, affecting ordination?*

The tradition of the church to have an educated clergy has not been displaced, but it has faced challenges. There is now a hunger among many to see the church more energized, more relevant, more intergenerational, and more ethnically inclusive. Leaders who can bring about such changes are sometimes more valued by congregations than having a minister with a divinity school education or a formal ordination.

Ministers of the church, like all disciples, are called to love God with both mind and heart (Mark 12:28-30). Aspiring young ministers should want to prepare themselves as thoroughly as possible in the context of the Bible, church history and doctrine, and in understanding the mission of the church. It is also important to have good leadership and relational skills and a passion for the growth and welfare of the church.

And despite the latest trends, ordination will remain a sacred and special part of church life. But newly ordained ministers should be alert to heightened and varied expectations from churches seeking ministers who can provide leadership in addressing the desires of congregations for a wide outreach and greater variety in worship structures and styles.

6.   *I am currently a student in divinity school and have not as yet been formally ordained to the ministry. My best friend recently became engaged and has asked me to conduct his wedding. Can I do it since I am not ordained?*

Probably not, if the couple desire legal recognition of their marriage. Legal marriages are generally performed by magistrates or ordained ministers. State law regarding legal marriage may vary from state to state, but in most cases a non-ordained minister cannot sign a marriage license if state law requires that an ordained minister conduct the ceremony. There are no doubt other ways you can participate in the service for your friend.

7.   *Is there a personal word of counsel you would offer to those considering ordination?*

As an ordained minister, I have been inspired and challenged by a statement I read in an excellent book by L. Gregory Jones and Kevin R. Armstrong titled *Resurrecting Excellence: Shaping Faithful Christian Ministry*. In a discussion regarding the need for excellence in ministry, the authors quote John Wimmer, who observed that in ministry today "there is a lot of mediocrity masquerading as faithfulness."[9]

This observation has challenged me to strive for excellence in the ministries I render. I do not want to be among those ministers who have succumbed to doing only what needs to be done. So the word of pastoral counsel I would offer to those seeking ordination is not to settle for mediocrity in discharging your duties in ministry. Come to the ordination experience with a commitment to excellence in the work you will do for God and the church. Honor God, who called you, with the offering of excellent work.

So, Should I Pursue Ordination?

This chapter has presented a picture of ordination and its meaning for the church and minister. God gives the church leadership to help it serve in the world. The purpose of ordination is to set apart those called by God to serve him, the church, and others.

Once ordination is understood, the next step is to assess one's readiness to move forward with the ordination process. The following questions may be helpful in assessing this readiness. They may also be helpful in further discussions with family, pastors, or mentors regarding a timetable to seek ordination. Affirmative answers to the questions suggest a positive inclination toward pursuing ordination.

1. *Are you sensing that ordination is calling you and that the timing is right to proceed with plans to be ordained?*

One of the best motivations for ordination is a sense of being led or compelled toward it. If this feeling is within you, this is good news. The timing may be right to proceed with ordination if all requirements, qualifications, and procedures have been met and satisfied. Are you eager and passionate about becoming an ordained minister of the church?

2. *Are you educationally prepared for ordination?*

Competence for the work is to be valued above enthusiasm for the moment. If more time is needed for educational preparation, it would be wise to postpone ordination until the education desired is achieved. Do not hesitate to talk to a respected pastor, professor, or mentor about this matter. Any of them will be eager to offer assistance. Think long term about your ministry aspirations.

3. *Have you experienced confirmation of your decision through prayer and the counsel of trusted friends and mentors?*

If so, this is a strong indication that you should proceed toward ordination. To have a conviction of heart and mind from the Holy Spirit coupled with the affirmation from those you respect is a powerful sign of the correctness of your decisions.

4. *Do your family and closest loved ones support your decision to be ordained?*

Family and spousal support are important elements in a decision to be ordained and should be evident at the time of ordination. Do not hesitate to delay plans for ordination until your family supports your decision. Time may improve matters. Family support and excitement at the time of ordination are large blessings. Lacking this support does not mean you should not be ordained. It does mean, however, that you should proceed cautiously and thoughtfully.

5. *Are all moral and ethical matters in your life in good order?*

There are no moral or ethical requirements for ordained clergy that are not expected of all Christians. Certain denominations or religious traditions may have specific ethical guidelines they wish to stress or a code of ethics for the minister to sign upon ordination.

Once ordained, the minister becomes an official representative of the church. Because ordained ministers represent the church, sins of the clergy are especially grievous. Although you are not expected to be a perfect person upon ordination, you should "do your best to present yourself to God as one approved by him, a worker who has no need to be ashamed…" (2 Tim. 2:15).

6. *Have you satisfied all requirements for ordination of your denomination or tradition?*

Fulfilling the expectations listed in the previous questions may serve to answer this question. But other requirements may be specified by a particular denomination. Successfully passing an ordination council review, presbytery evaluation, or written exam for ordination are not matters to be taken lightly. Fulfilling ordination requirements should be a source of pride. Seek to complete them with distinction.

A Final Thought and Message

It is a noble calling to serve God as one of his ministers, whether in an ordained role or as a lay minister. Immeasurable joy can come to those who offer their lives in dedicated service to God and to others. Such service is, indeed, worth a life.

Ministers of Christ and the church know that they are participants in work that really matters. Motivation to do good work in ministry can often arise from the conviction that the biblical story of God's desire to redeem his people and the life and teachings of Jesus are of ultimate significance in people's lives. A challenge for ministers in every generation is to respond to God's call with a commitment to render excellent work in service to him. Whether you respond to God's call as an ordained minister of the church or as a lay minister, seek to give him the best of your spiritual gifts, dedicated service, and hard work.

There are many vocational joys that result from a life spent in ministry. This can certainly be true for ordained ministers. To have the privilege to preach God's word regularly and routinely, to serve with fellow believers in building up the church, to be the pastor baptizing new believers, or to be the minister who administers the Lord's Supper to a congregation—all are spiritual and vocational treasures beyond measure. How honored we can be when those hurt by life's experiences turn to us for counsel and prayer, or ask us to voice a Christian benediction for a loved one when death comes. What a privilege it is to serve as a minister for God to help and bless others.

Even though there may be times when the work wears you down, one dynamic of God's call is that it seldom goes away. With rest and perspective, there can come renewal and rededication to the joys of participating in the work to which you have been called.

All of God's ministers are challenged to maintain and nurture their personal spiritual lives and devotional times with God. There is no substitute for the spiritual strength, insight, and energy that emerges from these holy moments. They empower us for the work we are called to do and provide us with unexpected energy and new ideas for serving God.

May the words from Paul to Timothy become your testimony about calling and ordination: *I thank Christ Jesus our Lord, who has given me strength, that he considered me trustworthy, appointing me to his service* (1 Tim. 1:12).

It is worth a life!

Questions for Discernment

1. What are your current thoughts about being ordained? If ordained already, what point in this chapter resonated with you the most?

2. Which questions related to ordination resonated with you? Why?

3. What do you think the qualifications for ordination should be?

Notes

[1]Alton McEachern, *Set Apart for Service: Baptist Ordination Practices* (Nashville: Broadman Press, 1980), 56.

[2]Dennis Campbell, *Who Will Go for Us? An Invitation to Ordained Ministry* (Nashville: Abingdon Press, 1994), 16.

[3]Ibid., 60.

[4]John I. Durham, *Exodus*, vol. 3 of Word Biblical Commentary (Grand Rapids: Zondervan, 1992), 384.

[5]Ibid., 63.

[6]McEachern, *Set Apart for Service*, 20-22.

[7]Ibid., 29.

[8]Daniel Aleshire, "A Commission to Students" (Sermon, Campbell University Divinity School, September 2003).

[9]L. Gregory Jones and Kevin R. Armstrong, *Resurrecting Excellence: Shaping Faithful Christian Ministry* (Grand Rapids: Eerdmans Publishing Company, 2006), 2.

Selected Bibliography

Ashcraft, Morris, ed. *God-Called Ministry: Essays on the Christian Ministry.* Cary, NC: Baptist State Convention of North Carolina, 1983.

Buechner, Frederick. *Wishful Thinking: A Seeker's ABC.* New York: HarperOne, 1994.

Campbell, Dennis. *Who Will Go For Us? An Invitation to Ordained Ministry.* Nashville: Abingdon Press, 1994.

Cullinan, Alice. Sorting It Out: Discerning God's Call to Ministry. Valley Forge, PA: Judson Press, 1999.

Dobbins, Kathy, Colin Harris, and Doris Nelms, eds., *Klesis: God's Call and Journey of Faith.* Atlanta: Cooperative Baptist Fellowship, 2005.

Francisco, Clyde. *Introducing the Old Testament, Revised Edition.* Nashville: Broadman Press, 1997.

Hamrick, Terry. *Leadership in Constant Change: Embracing a New Missional Reality.* Atlanta: Cooperative Baptist Fellowship, 2012.

Honeycutt, Roy L. *Jeremiah: Witness Under Pressure.* Nashville: Convention Press, 1981.

Johnson, Ben Campbell. *Hearing God's Call: Ways of Discernment and Clergy.* Grand Rapids: Wm. B. Eerdmans Publishing Company, 2002.

Killinger, John. *The Ministry Life: 101 Tips for Young Ministers.* Macon, GA; Smyth & Helwys Publishing, Inc., 2013.

Koskela, Doug. *Calling and Clarity: Discovering What God Wants For Your Life.* Grand Rapids: Wm. B. Eerdmans Publishing Company, 2015.

Labberton, Mark. *Called: The Crisis and Promise of Following Jesus Today.* Westmont, IL: IVP Books, 2014.

McEachern, Alton H. *Set Apart For Service; Baptist Ordination Practices.* Nashville: Broadman Press, 1980.

Niebuhr, H. Richard. *The Purpose of the Church and Its Ministry.* New York: Harper and Row, 1956.

O'Connor, Elizabeth. *Cry Pain, Cry Hope: Thresholds to Purpose.* Waco: Word Books, 1987.

Paschal, George W. *A History of North Carolina Baptists: 1869-1956.* Raleigh, NC: Baptist State Convention of North Carolina. Volume 2, 1955.

Placher, William C. *Callings: Twenty Centuries of Christian Wisdom on Vocation.* Grand Rapids: Wm. B. Eerdmans Publishing Company, 2005.

Rohr, Richard. *What the Mystics Know.* New York: The Crossroads Publishing Company, 2015.

Schurmann, Douglas J. *Vocation: Discerning Our Vocation in Life.* Grand Rapids: Wm. B. Eerdmans Publishing Company, 2004.